OUR DYNAMIC WORLD: THE SERIES

CORE
All students must cover Book 1 (Workbook highly recommended)

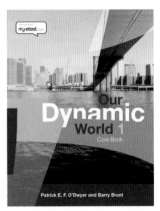

Book 1: covers the core sections of the syllabus which must be taken by all students

A workbook to accompany *Our Dynamic World 1*

ELECTIVES
All students must cover *either* Book 2 *or* Book 3

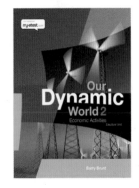

Book 2: Economic Activities – Elective Unit

Book 3: The Human Environment – Elective Unit

OPTIONS
Higher Level only students cover *either* Book 4 *or* Book 5

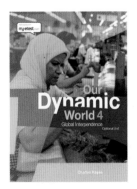

Higher level only

 OR

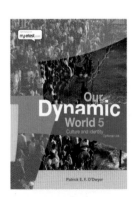

Book 4: Global Interdependence – Optional Unit

Book 5: Culture and Identity – Optional Unit

OUR DYNAMIC WORLD

CULTURE AND IDENTITY

PATRICK N. DWYER

My-etest

Packed full of extra questions, **my-etest** lets you revise –
at your own pace – when you want – where you want.
Test yourself on our FREE website www.my-etest.com and check
out how well you score!

Teachers!

Print an etest and give it for homework or a class test.

GILL & MACMILLAN

Gill & Macmillan Ltd
Hume Avenue
Park West
Dublin 12
with associated companies throughout the world
www.gillmacmillan.ie

© Patrick O'Dwyer 2004
0 7171 3586 1
Design, colour illustration and print origination in Ireland by Design Image, Dublin
Colour repro by Ultragraphics, Dublin

*The paper used in this book is made from the wood pulp of managed forests. For every tree felled,
at least one tree is planted, thereby renewing natural resources.*

'Skinheads convicted of German race murder' on p. 81 reprinted with permission of
The Associated Press.

OPTIONAL UNIT: CULTURE AND IDENTITY

	Content description	National settings	International settings

1	**Statement:**
	Populations can be examined according to physical and cultural indicators. Culture and identity are tied to ideas of ethnicity, which include race, language, religion, and nationality. (chapters 1–15)
	
	Students should study:
	• racial groupings within the global population to include
	  – characteristics and locational patterns
	  – multi-racial societies
	  – racial mixing
	  – racial conflict
	• an understanding of the impact of colonialism and migration on racial patterns
	• language as a cultural indicator and include
	  – major language groups
	  – European languages – influence of the mass-media
	  – minority languages – policies for survival
	• religion as a cultural indicator and include
	  – the distribution of major world religions
	  – the relationship between church and state
	  – religious conflict
	• everyday expressions of culture and identity, e.g. sports, traditions, costumes, food, music, art and festivals.
		Asylum seekers and refugees.
		
		Irish language Gaeltacht areas.
		
		Irish constitution.
		Northern Ireland.
		
		Irish examples.
			Appropriate European and global examples.
			
			Appropriate examples, e.g. Welsh.
			
			Appropriate European examples.

2	**Statement:** **Nationality and the nation state are political entities placed on the physical and cultural landscape. (chapters 16–20)** Students should study the complex issues relating to: • physical and political boundaries • examples of cultural groups within nation states • examples of cultural groups without nationality • conflicts between political structures and cultural groups.	The island of Ireland and partition. Northern Ireland.	Appropriate examples.

	Content description	National settings	International settings

3	Statement:
	Identity as a concept entails a variety of cultural factors including nationality, language, race, and religion.
	(chapter 21)
	
	Students should study:
	• a case study of a European region to draw together the issues of race, nationality, and identity already discussed. This should include an examination of
	  – historical developments: physical and political boundaries
	  – ethnicity and race
	  – religion
	  – music, art, festivals etc
	  – the role of migration
	  – new boundaries
			An appropriate case study e.g. Celtic regions, The Balkans or Switzerland.

CONTENTS

ACKNOWLEDGMENTS

The author wishes to thank the following people for their help and advice during the production of this script.

Special thanks are due to Hubert Mahony, educational publishing director, for his constant expert advice and support. Thanks also to managing editor Tess Tattersall, editor Kate Duffy, photo researcher Helen Thompson, and the staff at Gill & Macmillan for their tireless work behind the scenes.

Sincere thanks to Dara O'Doherty and her team at Design Image for their creative and elegant design of this book.

INTRODUCTION

CULTURE AND IDENTITY

The term culture, like the term identity, is very difficult to define. The two are intimately associated, for every culture possesses a particular and very often very different identity.

A culture may be defined as a total way of life of a people or group. The combination of ideas, beliefs, institutions (organisations), skills and tools possessed by a group may form its culture. In addition, it is important to understand that culture is seldom if ever stagnant; it is usually in a state of change. It is dynamic. New ideas are added over time, while some traditions fade away and are replaced by new ones.

It is culture that creates identity, that makes a person feel part of a group with whom they share a common way of life, experiences, traits and traditions. These common factors may be shared by people over a region of the earth's surface. These areas are called cultural regions. Some are small, such as Gaeltacht regions, while others across North Africa, Arabia and the Middle East are very large. Another large cultural region is the Indian Realm in South Asia.

This book attempts to examine certain regions of the world where culture and identity are associated with ideas of ethnicity, language, religion, nationality and home. These factors affect different groups and nations with whom they come into contact.

Where possible, this book attempts to use examples and case studies of regions that are covered in the core text *Our Dynamic World 1* and electives.

SECTION 1
THE DYNAMICS OF POPULATION

KEY IDEA! Populations can be studied according to physical and cultural characteristics. Culture and identity are tied to ideas of ethnicity, which include race, language, religion and nationality.

Section 1 includes chapters 1–15. It explains the meaning of racial groups and their interactions. It deals with topics such as ethnicity, multiracial societies, racial mixing, racial conflict and an understanding of the impact of colonisation and migration on some ethnic groups.

It also investigates language and religion as cultural influences, which often lead to conflict between different ethnic or religious groups.

Some religions are associated with certain world regions. On occasion religious conflict may occur between some religious groups.

The world's population has many ethnic groups who identify with different cultures and traditions.

Conflict occurs in some areas between cultural groups and nation-states.

CHAPTER 1
RACIAL AND ETHNIC GROUPS

THE MEANING OF RACE

The word race gives rise to much misunderstanding. Many people associate race with factors such as language, religion and nationality. These are cultural factors and can be changed by anyone if they so wish. Racial character, on the other hand, cannot be changed.

One's race or racial character cannot be changed because it is fixed for us at conception – we are born with it. In other words, race is simply **biological inheritance**. Race refers to **physical characteristics**, such as skin colour, height, hair type, physique and shape of head. Scientists call these characteristics physical traits; they are passed on through genes from parent to offspring.

See Chapter 7 in
Our Dynamic World 3.

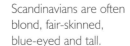
Scandinavians are often blond, fair-skinned, blue-eyed and tall.

Is there such a thing as a pure race?

Simply, there is no such thing as a pure race. Widespread migration and intermingling of people leading to interbreeding between people of different continents has blurred all racial boundaries. For this reason, many scientists use the term 'ethnic group', which relates to race, in order to describe large groups of people having certain physical characteristics in common. While it is not true to speak of pure races, it is true that segregation and isolation lead to recognisable, fixed physical characteristics. For example:

- The people of Scandinavia form an especially distinctive group, fair-haired, fair-skinned, tall and blue-eyed. This may be explained by a combination of the area's relatively isolated position and its northern latitude. Also, historically, people have moved out of rather than into Scandinavia. In other words it was an area of out migration rather than in migration. Push factors were stronger than pull factors, and so there was less intermingling with outside groups.
- The Aborigines of Australia were cut off, on this once isolated continent, for so long that as a group they remain physically and genetically distinctive.
- The Kalahari Bush people were similarly isolated in the semi-arid region of south-west Africa.

Kalahari Bush people share many similar characteristics.

Australian Aborigines lived on an isolated continent and so are racially distinctive.

SKIN COLOUR AND RACE

Initially, the human race was divided according to skin colour, the most obvious physical characteristic. Five groups were recognised: white, yellow, red, brown and black. Even though this was an easy way to do things, it was neither satisfactory nor scientific. For instance, both the sub-Saharan Africans and the Aborigines have very dark skin, but they belong to two distinct ethnic groups.

Skin colour has been the excuse for huge amounts of inhumanity for thousands of years. Today's scientists believe that, initially, dark-coloured and light-coloured skin evolved because of humans **adapting to environments**, such as hot sunny climates and cooler cloudier climates. **Because** humans adapted **they survived** and their offspring **passed** on these **traits** through their **genes**.

It is believed that skin colour is a result of the presence of a molecule called **melanin. We all have the same number of melanin-producing cells.** However, in dark-skinned people these cells produce forty-three times more melanin per cell than light-skinned people produce. **Because it is 'an amount thing', interbreeding between races results in a wide range of shades of colour.**

When humans lost their covering of body hair they would have been vulnerable to the effects of ultraviolet light. Melanin is necessary to combat the effects of ultraviolet (UV) light by absorbing these dangerous rays and so protects against cancer. The greater the intensity of light the greater is the need for melanin. So groups near the tropics needed greater amounts of this substance than groups who later lived at higher latitudes, and so became dark-skinned. In addition dark skin was essential to combat the effects of light on the production of **folic acid** that is essential if people are **to remain fertile** and to produce healthy offspring.

Humans need some **UV light to create vitamin D₃**. Because there is less UV light available at higher latitudes than lower latitudes **some humans developed genes for** creating **lighter-coloured skin.** Those that adapted to this requirement survived and passed on their genes to their offspring. Those that could not adapt died off, as they would have developed **rickets** due to lack of vitamin D₃, which at that time would have been fatal.

So when you see skin colour in terms of this balancing act scientists can predict, from knowing the amount of UV light that reaches the earth's surface at different latitudes, an optimal skin colour (or melanin content) for peoples living at those latitudes.

Can you explain the difference between 'culture' and 'race'?

The development of dark skin was essential to survival in tropical latitudes.

The development of vitamin D₃ was more essential to the survival of northern Europeans than the risk of cancer.

More genetic differences may exist between these differing Irish teenagers than between this Indian and these Irish youngsters.

SKIN COLOUR AND GENETIC MAKE-UP

Class activity

1. Explain why there is no such thing as a pure race. In your answer refer to:
   - migration;
   - skin colour
   - genetic make-up.
2. Explain how the need to survive led to the variations in human skin colour.

Of all the genes in humans, about 75 per cent are identical in every person, **only 25 per cent vary from person to person.** Of that 25 per cent difference, about 85 per cent would be present even if two people were fairly closely related, such as the ethnic subgroup of Norwegians (Norwegians are a subgroup of Caucasians or Europeans). Another 9 per cent would be present from being members of separate nations or tribes (e.g. a Spaniard and an Italian). Only about 6 per cent of the difference is the result of the two people being, from what we call, separate races. So any person's race accounts for only about 1.5 per cent (or 6 per cent of 25 per cent) of his genetic make-up. This means that far more genetic differences exist between people of the same race than between different races.

Anthropologists differ amongst themselves as to how many distinct ethnic groups there are, but most recognise five or six groups.

1. Caucasoid (white, Caucasian): Europeans and people of European ancestry, brown-skinned peoples such as Arabs, and people of the Indian subcontinent

2. Northern, Central and East Asian: Chinese, Inuit, Samis and American Indians (Amerindians)

3. Africans and black people of African descent (Afro-Americans)

4. Black Australian Aborigines

Identify the physical characteristics of the people in each of these photographs.

5. The Bush people of the Kalahari Desert

CHAPTER 2
RACIAL LOCATION PATTERNS AND RACIAL CHARACTERISTICS

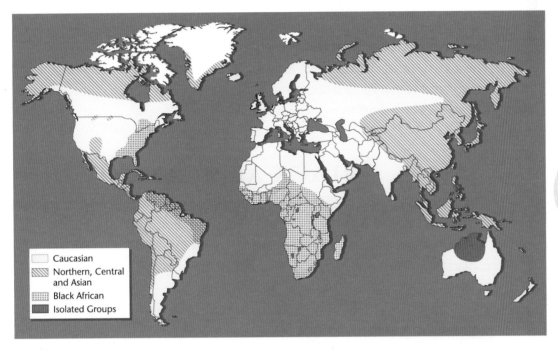

Fig. 2.1

Caucasian
Northern, Central and Asian
Black African
Isolated Groups

This is a generalised map of racial distribution. The fact that many black people live all along the Brazilian east coast and many whites of Spanish descent live all along the west coast of South America is not shown here.

CAUCASIANS

Caucasians are the most widespread racial group. This group occupies a broad zone across America and from the Atlantic coasts of Europe and North Africa to the Indian Ocean and the Bay of Bengal and filters up into central Asia. Other Caucasians are found from eastern Brazil south to Argentina and Chile, Australia, New Zealand and South Africa.

Caucasians are found scattered throughout the world because Europeans colonised many regions.

General racial characteristics

The general racial characteristics include: fair to brown skin, light to brown hair which is straight to wavy, light blue to brown eyes, and medium to tall in height. The group is thought to have evolved in the general area of the Caucasus Mountains between the Caspian Sea and the Black Sea. The Caucasian group may be subdivided into three sub-groups, the Nordic group, the Alpine group and the Mediterranean group. The Nordic group are mainly the people of Scandinavia who are especially distinctive: fair hair, blue eyes, high cheek bones and tall.

Identify the characteristics of this Scandinavian person.

Remember, there is no such thing as a pure race.
Name two countries in east Asia.
Name two countries in south Asia.

Identify the characteristics of these Chinese people.

An Inuit hunter

Identify the physical characteristics of the people in each of these photos.

NORTH, CENTRAL AND EAST ASIAN

People from central, east, south-east and north Asia mainly have light brown skin, darkening southwards in Malaysia and Indonesia, which may reflect the effect of increased sun. Inuit belong to this group. After Asian people crossed the Bering Strait, from Siberia to Alaska, they moved south through North and South America. Their descendants, the American Indians (Amerindians) belong to this ethnic group.

General racial characteristics

The general racial characteristics include: light brown or reddish-brown skin, a broad head with a flat face and nose, straight and coarse black to brown hair, brown eyes and short to medium height.

BLACK AFRICAN

Most of the black African people live south of the Sahara. Other regions include the United States, the Caribbean Islands, Brazil and Britain.

Some people from East Africa have a more mixed set of characteristics as contact with Arab and Indian traders indicates racial mixing.

Young Zulu females

An African-American family

General racial characteristics

The general racial characteristics include black to brown skin, long head with projecting jaw, black to dark brown hair of a coarse texture and dark eyes. The most distinctive black features occur amongst the people of West Africa. These features become less distinctive as distance increases from this core region.

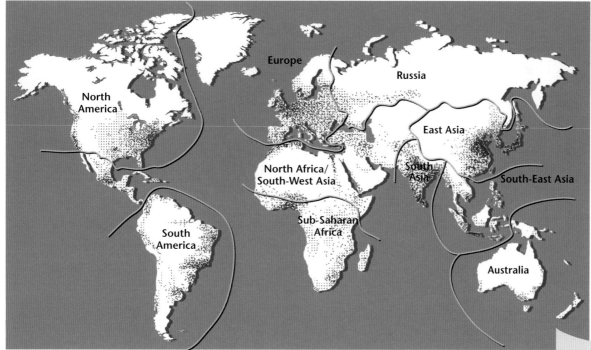

Fig. 2.2
East Asia: the world's greatest population cluster is concentrated in the valleys and flood plains of China's major rivers.
South Asia: centred on India, Bangladesh and Pakistan. This cluster of people will overtake East Asia early in the twenty-first century.
Europe: the world's third largest population cluster lies on the same landmass as East Asia and South Asia but at the opposite end on the Atlantic coastline.
East Asia, South Asia and **Europe** account for 3.4 billion of the world's 6.1 billion people.

This population density map will give you some idea of the relative numbers of people there are in each of the racial groups.

POINTS TO REMEMBER ABOUT MIGRATION LEADING TO PRESENT RACIAL AND CULTURAL MIXING

Examples of migration through time include:

● The movement of the Islamic Moors across North Africa from Arabia and northward into Europe via Spain, into Central Asia via Turkey and into the Balkans;

● The movement on an unprecedented scale of Europeans to North and South America;

● British to Africa, Australia, and New Zealand;

● Africans to North and South America;

● Indians (from what is today India/Pakistan/Bangladesh) to East Africa, South-east Asia, the Caribbean, Fiji – all parts of the British Empire;

● Chinese throughout South-east Asia;

● Jews from Europe to Israel;

● Americans and Canadians westward across the North American continent;

● Russians eastward across the Asian continent;

● Mexicans northward to the US;

● Vietnamese, Central Americans, Cubans, Haitians to the USA.

Class activity
1. Explain why South Asia has such a high population density.
2. Explain why Brazil, the Caribbean Islands and the eastern United States have a high population of people of black African descent.
3. Use a physical map of China to explain why most Chinese people live along its eastern regions.

Migration has had a significant effect on world geography.

- It has contributed to the evolution and development of separate cultures.
- It has contributed to the spread of cultures by interchange and communication.
- It has contributed to the complex mix of people and cultures found in different regions of the world today.

Research Islamic Moors and the reasons for this migration.

How has migration influenced the creation of new music sounds and lyrics such as 'rap' – can you name others?

THE IMPACT OF EUROPE UPON WORLD MIGRATION AND RACIAL PATTERNS

Overview

The colonisation of the New World was the key factor in the development of European prosperity. Firstly, emigration to the New World was a release valve for countries to transport surplus population and so remove unemployed and landless people from European countries. For example, one-third of the population growth in the USA between 1850 and 1910 came from the immigration of working-age people from Europe. But for Europeans, the rest of the world was much more important than just providing areas for overflow population, and the impact of Europeans on the rest of the world was much greater than just as migrants. The European-settled lands of North America, Australia and New Zealand, parts of South America and South Africa, provided cheap food for Europe's growing population and raw materials for its industries.

Americans are of mixed ancestry.

Many native Indian people died of diseases that were carried by the conquistadors to the Americas.

However, the effect of European migration was much less beneficial and sometimes devastating for those areas and their peoples affected by European colonisation. In North and South America the effects of European contact were catastrophic, particularly in Central and South America which were much more densely populated than the North. In Mexico, for example, estimates vary. One estimate suggests a decline from 25 million people in 1519 (although other estimates puts this figure at 10 million) to just over 1 million by the end of that century, recovering to just under 4 million by the end of the eighteenth century. The native American people of what is now the USA are believed to have declined from about 5 million in 1500 to 60,000 three centuries later. These native peoples were devastated by epidemics of infectious diseases – smallpox, measles, influenza, tuberculosis and chickenpox – against which they had no immunity, as well as by genocide and the effects of forced labour.

Forced migration to the new colonies in the USA, Caribbean and Brazil where labour was needed to work the sugar and cotton plantations began in the fifteenth century and reached its peak in the seventeenth and eighteenth centuries. In some areas, such as Brazil, it lasted until the nineteenth century. It has been estimated that some 10 million slaves were imported from Africa into the New World and that perhaps as many as 2 million more died on the sea journey. The population and cultural impact on West Africa especially, was immense. Depopulation followed, not only as a result of loss of people through slavery, but also as a consequence of the political and social disorganisation which followed.

Look up 'The Slave Trade' on the web for more information.

In Asia, colonisation resulted in little permanent settlement. However, the development of tin mines and rubber plantations led to large-scale migration of people, such as Chinese and Indians, to work in places such as Malaysia. Chinese form 28 per cent and Indians form 8 per cent of the Malaysian population.

The process of colonialism and the growth of capitalism have created a global labour market (a worldwide source of workers) which has driven migration movements. **At the end of the twentieth and the beginning of the twenty-first centuries the uneven economic development of countries worldwide has accelerated these migration patterns.** While many migrants, especially those with skills, choose to move in search of a better life elsewhere, others are forced to do so by political and economic pressures. Post-colonial unrest (civil wars, coups), oppressive regimes (government, dictators) in Iran, Iraq and Afghanistan, wars in south and south-east Asia as well as in Africa, Colombia in South America, eastern European countries and the former Soviet Union, have all generated large-scale migration, both legal and illegal (in the form of human trafficking) into the West or neighbouring countries. **The UN estimates that the number of refugees worldwide at present is 21.5 million.**

Many African people were forced to work as slaves on plantations in American colonies.

Such **migration has created fears that the distinctiveness of individual nations is under threat**, and so too is the nation-state. Across Europe legal and illegal migrants (especially those that are non-white) are being identified as a threat to the economic and cultural well-being of nation-states because they are regarded as a drain on the welfare state and as polluting national culture. For example, the recent rise in the number of people seeking asylum in Europe has been met with hostility in Ireland and Britain. Government debates and popular media scares about bogus asylum-seekers living on the welfare state represent little more than thinly veiled racism.

Many Europeans were displaced from their homes as a result of civil war during the 1990s.

Class activity
Explain how colonisation affected racial distribution in each of the following regions:
North America; South America; Asia; Australia: Africa.

TEST YOURSELF AT
my-etest.com

CHAPTER 3
MULTIRACIAL SOCIETIES

Many European countries, such as Britain, the Netherlands, Spain and France were once colonial powers. Consequently, many former citizens of these colonies now live in these countries.

BRITAIN – A MULTIRACIAL SOCIETY

Britain had many colonies. Carefully study Fig. 3.1. It shows the extent of the British Empire. Then identify the various racial ethnic/groups that lived within these colonial regions.

> Ethnic or ethnicity refers to a minority group with a collective self-identity within a larger host nation.

> So, which distinct racial groups are found in Britain? Use the map as one source of information.

Activity

1. Identify, in rank order, the various ethnic groups in Britain.
2. Explain why South Asians form the largest ethnic group in Britain.

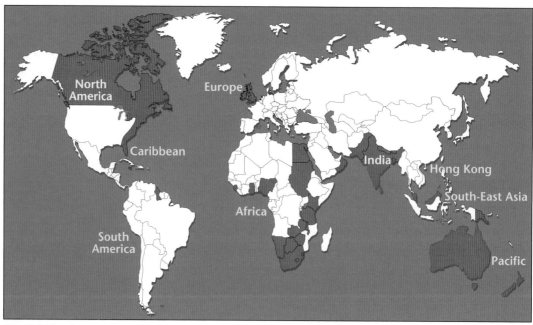

Fig. 3.1 The former colonies of the British Empire

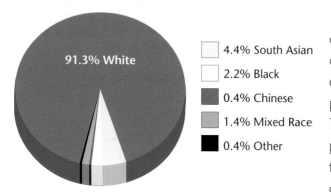

91.3% White

☐ 4.4% South Asian
☐ 2.2% Black
☐ 0.4% Chinese
☐ 1.4% Mixed Race
■ 0.4% Other

Fig. 3.2

The ethnic or multiracial population in Great Britain has evolved from mass immigration of people from former British colonies in the Caribbean and South Asian sub-continent during the 1950s and 1960s. Ethnic minorities make up 8.8 per cent of the population of Great Britain, and account for 7.2 per cent of all people of working age in 2000. South Asian people consisting of Indians, Bangladeshis and Pakistanis are the largest ethnic minority group. They make up 4.4 per cent of the population; followed by black people from the Caribbean and Africans who make up 2.2 per cent; the

Chinese make up 0.4 per cent of the population. People from ethnic minorities remain concentrated in the larger urban areas, especially in Greater London, and in some cases form a majority of the local population in certain districts, such as Notting Hill.

At the peak of immigration in 1961, before the Commonwealth Immigrants Act came into effect in 1962, some 50,000 people arrived from the West Indies in one year. The migration was in fact encouraged from the Caribbean by the offer of employment from London Transport and the National Health Service.

Class activity
1. Which region of Britain has the highest percentage of minorities?
2. Explain the pattern in the distribution of minority groups. (Why are they in some regions and not in others?) In your answer refer to: England; Scotland; Wales.

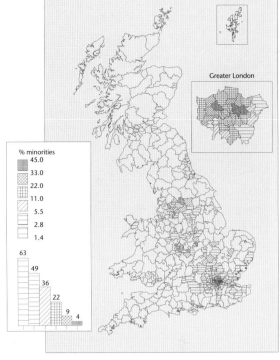

Fig. 3.3 Distribution of minority ethnic groups in Britain.

Britain was the centre of the triangular traffic whereby British ships took goods to Africa. These goods were exchanged for slaves. Then the same British ships transported the slaves to the Caribbean and North America before returning home with industrial raw materials such as cotton. The majority of these slaves worked in the plantations of the Caribbean and North America. But some came to Britain to be personal household servants. Over time, they intermarried with native-born Britons.

Do you remember mercantilism from your Junior Certificate course?

FRANCE – A MULTIRACIAL SOCIETY

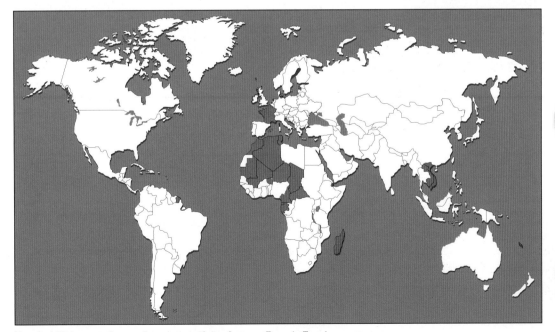

Fig. 3.4 This map shows the extent of the former French Empire.

Carefully study this map of the former French Empire. Then identify the countries highlighted that formed part of this region.

Which of these countries form part of sub-Saharan Africa?

French citizens include many people from its former colonies.

Like Great Britain, France was a former colonial power. The French state keeps few immigration statistics beyond the numbers of foreign-born migrants legally resident in France or who have become French citizens (about 4 million). There is no official figure for the total number of French residents of foreign background, nor any breakdown of where they come from, but it is estimated that about 14 million French citizens, nearly one-quarter of the total population have at least an immigrant parent or grandparent.

A large share of the post-war immigrants and their offspring come from former French colonies in North Africa, such as Algeria, Morocco and Tunisia; from countries in sub-Saharan Africa, such as Senegal; and from countries in south-east Asia, such as Kampuchea, Vietnam and Laos. Immigrants also came from colonies in the Caribbean, such as Guadeloupe and Martinique, and from French Guyana in South America. Much of this population is concentrated in the suburbs and urban centres such as Marseilles and Lyons. Most immigrants live in ghetto-like communities. In addition large past migrations and high birth rates among immigrants have made Islam France's second-largest religion.

Some ethnic groups prefer to live in cultural areas or ghettos of many French cities.

Many immigrants, especially those from Algeria and Morocco, came to France as 'guest workers' in the 1960s and 1970s. Migrants were seen as an asset for economic development within the core countries of the EU, such as France and Germany. Migrant workers performed jobs not wanted by the French, because the jobs were poorly paid, unpleasant, dirty or involved heavy manual work. The migrants were glad of employment and sent home much of their earnings to help their families' incomes. France was also pleased that such jobs were being done while French citizens could accept better paid and higher quality jobs.

In France, all citizens are deemed equal and indistinguishable in relation to the state. Be their origins Algerian, Senegalese or Corsican, French citizens are deemed identical in their Frenchness. Unlike Britain or Ireland, where different ethnic or religious groups enjoy rights and recognition based on their minority status, the idea of such distinctions is against France's traditional thinking. 'In France, once you are French, you are French and that's it.'

However, mass migration since the 1950s from sub-Saharan countries is putting this ideal to the test.

Class activity
1. Explain how the influence of French colonialism differed from that of British colonialism in relation to the worldwide distribution of ethnic groups.
2. Explain why the influence of French citizenship helps reduce ethnic conflict within France.
3. Why did many migrants from former French colonies enter France after 1960?

TEST YOURSELF AT
my-etest.com

CHAPTER 4
RACIAL MIXING

Case Study: Brazil – a Cultural Melting Pot

Brazil's population of 167 million people is as diverse as that of the United States. Its native Amerindian people were drastically reduced following European colonisation. No more than 275,000 Amerindians now survive deep in the Amazon region.

There are about 80 million black people in Brazil. These are the descendants of the slaves brought by the Portuguese to work the sugar and cotton plantations along the north-east coast. Significantly, however, there has been much racial mixing, and 67 million Brazilians have combined European, African and some Amerindian ancestries. The remaining 91 million, now barely in the majority at 55 per cent, are mainly of European origin, the descendants of immigrants from Portugal, Italy, Germany and Eastern Europe. This complex society also has large numbers of Lebanese, Syrians and the largest community of ethnic Japanese outside of Japan. The Japanese now number 1.3 million and have filtered right to the top of Brazilian society.

Brazil stands apart from all other nations by its progress in dealing with its racial divisions. Black people are still the least advantaged, but ethnic mixing is so common that hardly any group is unaffected and official statistics about 'Blacks' and 'Whites' is almost meaningless.

However, in its hunger for land, many Amerindians (native Americans) have been forced off their lands and into reservations by the Brazilian government. This has occurred because the government does not recognise ownership rights to the traditional tribal lands of the Amazonian Indians, rather than because of racial bias towards them.

Brazil's mixed population:

- Amerindians – native Indian tribes
- Mestizos – people of mixed European and Indian origin
- Blacks – people of African origin
- Whites – people of European origin
- Mulattos – people of mixed white and black origin
- Asian – people of south-east Asia and Japan

Brazil has one of the most racially diverse populations in the world. It is called 'a melting pot' of races.

What evidence in this picture of the Brazilian World Cup winning team indicates Brazil is a cultural melting pot?

Fig. 4.1 Identify the African countries where slaves were captured and subsequently transported to the Americas during the slave trade.

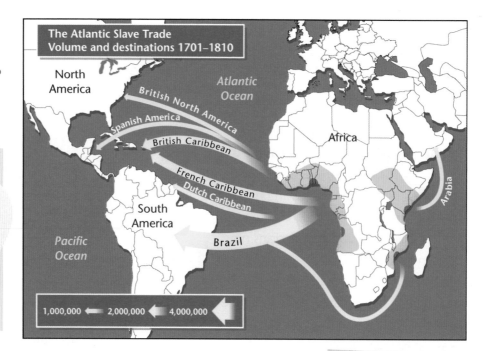

The Atlantic Slave Trade
Volume and destinations 1701–1810

North America

Atlantic Ocean

British North America

Spanish America

British Caribbean

French Caribbean

Dutch Caribbean

Africa

Arabia

South America

Pacific Ocean

Brazil

1,000,000 ← 2,000,000 ← 4,000,000

Using the scale of this flow chart identify the numbers of West Africans that were transported to:
- Brazil
- Caribbean
- North America

Activities

Carefully study this extract and then do the following:

1. Explain why Brazil has such a mixed racial population.
2. Explain some advantages of living in a multicultural society such as Brazil.
3. Explain the advantages and disadvantages for black people who live in Brazil.
4. Is racial discrimination active in Brazil? Explain.
5. Use the web to research Brazil's music and dance.

It is over 500 years since the Portuguese colonised Brazil. This 500-year anniversary has made Brazilians think about their origins, the racial mix of Indians, Africans and Europeans which has produced today's population and the claim that Brazil is a racial democracy. No other country outside Africa has such a large black population, about half of the total of 160 million people, yet blacks are almost totally absent from positions of power – from all levels of government, from congress, senate, the judiciary, the higher ranks of the civil service and the armed forces. Even in Salvador, the major slave port for nearly 300 years, where blacks make up more than 80 per cent of the population, very few are found in its local government.

A rights group reported in 2000 that racial discrimination is active in Brazil. Black and mixed-race Brazilians still have higher infant mortality rates, fewer years of schooling, higher rates of unemployment and earn less for the same work. Black men are more likely to be shot or arrested as crime suspects, and when found guilty, get longer sentences than white men. Yet there is no black movement in Brazil, no open racial conflict, no apparent racial tension. Black Americans who live in Salvador say they feel much more at ease there than in the racially divided USA. One of the reasons for this huge difference between the USA and Brazil is that while in America, race is defined by your ancestors – one drop of black blood makes you black – in Brazil what counts is your appearance. If you look white, or whitish, then you are white. For black Brazilians it is this very blurring of racial-lines that makes it so difficult to fight racism. And paradoxically, offers the chance for Brazil to become a real racial democracy, once it faces up to and takes steps to combat racism.

By Jan Rocha

Racial Mixing in the United States of America

The African-American group is the only group to have involuntarily immigrated to the United States. A recent survey indicated that while nearly two-thirds of whites thought that race relations would eventually improve, only 44 per cent of blacks agreed.

One way by which the 'American melting pot' works is through the intermarriages of different racial, ethnic and national groups. Only one-quarter of non-Hispanic (not of Spanish blood) whites was married to someone with an undivided ethnic heritage identical to his or her own. For instance, in the case of Italian-Americans: of those born before 1920, some 8 per cent had mixed ancestry, compared to over 70 per cent of those born after 1970.

The melting pot has not, however, welded that many unions across racial lines. Roughly 99 per cent of African-American women and 97 per cent of African-American men marry one of their ethnic group. This is not to take away from the fact that for every 100,000 married couples in the United States, in 2000 there were over 400 black-white unions compared to 126 in 1960.

America is a multiracial society where racial mixing has been slow to occur.

Large numbers of black Americans live in ghetto communities with whom they share a common culture.

Some ghettos have come to symbolise the place of the underclass within the city. Some people believe that with no work, no income and no property the only way a young man can achieve a masculine identity and respect is through crime and gang membership. Through demonstrations of courage and power, they are able to produce notions of working-class masculinity.

Class activity

1. Is marriage between racial groups common in the USA?
2. Identify one anti-social activity associated with young males in deprived urban regions of American cities.
3. Explain why such anti-social behaviour occurs.

Research some information on the Civil Rights Movement in the United States. Also some active racist groups such as the Ku Klux Klan.

Consider that it was only in November 2000 that, after a state election, Alabama became the last state to overturn a law that prohibited blacks and whites from marrying.

See 'Ghettos', Chapter 17 of *Our Dynamic World 3*.

TEST YOURSELF AT

my-etest.com

15

CHAPTER 5
RACIAL CONFLICT

Racial conflict is a pressing problem of our modern world. Many struggles and wars continue because of inbred fears and prejudices passed on from one generation to the next. Important examples of racial conflict include apartheid in South Africa and the Holocaust in Germany.

To recap on apartheid or the Holocaust look at *Our Dynamic World 3*, page 50.

Case Study: Racial Conflict in the United States

- At the end of World War II, Americans showed increasing concern over racial discrimination. In the South segregation laws separated the ethnic groups in public schools and prevented blacks from entering restaurants, theatres and other public places reserved only for whites. In the North, where no segregation laws existed, blacks still faced discrimination in buying homes and seeking jobs. Many national leaders, both black and white, emphasised the need to end racial discrimination and to guarantee to blacks their civil rights.

- In the South, especially in the states of Alabama and Mississippi, violence against blacks by whites was rarely fully investigated. Blacks felt they were not protected by the law and were sometimes subjected to brutal beatings and many were murdered by racist groups such as the Ku Klux Klan (KKK).

- Violence and racial tension occurred. Most civil rights' demonstrations stressed non-violence. But the demonstrations sometimes caused tension that resulted in violence. Violence increased as the civil rights' campaign intensified. Martin Luther King, the black leader of the Civil Rights Movement, who was a Nobel peace-prize winner, was assassinated.

Class activity

Write an essay on social discrimination in the United States. In your essay, use examples and refer specifically to the black minority group. Use as many sources of material as you can.

Marches created tension that often led to violence by police.

Martin Luther King, like Gandhi, preached peaceful protest.

The Ku Klux Klan is a racist group in the United States.

Watch the film *Mississippi Burning.* This will give you some idea of the racial conflict that existed in the United States.

- City ghettos bred unrest. Because of discrimination in the selling and renting of housing, many blacks were denied the right to live where they chose. Such unrest led to the Black Panther Movement.

Search the web for information on the Black Panther Movement.

RACIAL CONFLICT IN INDIA

Racial conflict in India may be looked at under two headings:
- The caste system in India
- Northern and southern Indians

The Caste System

The word caste is not a word native to India. It comes from the **Portuguese word** *castra* which means family, race, strain or breed. It usually refers to the groups of society into which the people of India are divided by religious laws. But in a general sense it means a **hereditary division** of any society into classes **on the basis of occupation, colour, wealth or religion**.

India has four castes. The highest-ranking group are the Brahmans. **All others who do not belong** to any of these four groups become outcasts or **untouchables**. Due to the work of some leaders, such as Mahatma Gandhi, new laws passed in 1955 granted full social standing to untouchables and any discrimination against them became a punishable crime.

To fully appreciate the caste system one has to look at the religious beliefs that are an integral part of it. The concern of a true Hindu is not his ranking in terms of wealth within society, but rather his ability to be reborn into a higher existence during each successive life. Simply a Hindu believes 'everything lies in the hand of God. We hope to go to the top, but our Karma (action) binds us to this level.' This refers to the concept of reincarnation. To the colonists, the British, the caste system appeared to be a static system of social division (as was the case in Britain), that allowed the ruling class or Brahmins, to maintain their power over other classes.

With the **introduction** of European and particularly **British systems** to India, the caste system began to change. It was a natural reaction of Indians attempting to adjust to the new regime and to make the most of whatever opportunities may have been presented to them. So, **the castes became rigid social divisions**. No-one could rise to a higher caste than the one into which one was born. Consequently, no marriages took place between castes. The Hindu legal code, called the **code of Manu**, said that a person would be born again into a higher caste, if he lived righteously and followed the code rigidly.

The caste system is a form of racial discrimination.

Recent advances in education are reducing the impact of the caste system, especially in the cities.

The Hindus' acceptance of their lot is not terribly different from the aim of the poor in Western society. The aim of the poor in the West is to improve their lot in the space of a single lifetime. The aim of the lower castes in India is to improve their position over the space of many lifetimes.

India, today, has become more flexible in its caste system's customs. In general, urban people are less strict about the caste system than rural people. In cities, different caste people intermarry and mingle with each other. In some rural areas there is still **discrimination based on castes** and on people being **untouchables**. Sometimes in villages and cities there are violent clashes that are connected to caste tensions. Although laws have changed, most of the communities who were low in the caste hierarchy remain low in the social order even today, even though the economic status of some may have changed. And communities who were high in social ranking remain high today. Most of the degrading jobs are still done by the Dalits or untouchables, while the Brahmans remain at the top of the hierarchy by being doctors, engineers and lawyers.

> Why, do you think, is discrimination more common in rural areas than urban areas?

A light-skinned person in northern India

Northern and Southern Indians

Over the past 1000 years, almost all racial and ethnic groups have passed through India, for it was the prime market of the world. All trade routes including the fabled silk route ended there. The people of India belong to **all the major racial groups**. However, **Caucasians make up 90 per cent of the population**. People of Asian descent live mainly in the Himalayan Mountains, the highlands of the north-east and central India.

The British ruled India, as they did other lands, by a divide and conquer strategy. They promoted religious, ethnic and cultural divisions among their colonists to keep them under their control. One cultural division they promoted was that India is a land of two races – the lighter-skinned Aryans, speaking a language of European origin (see Indo-European language page 27) in the northern half of the country and the darker-skinned Dravidians, who speak a different language, in the southern half. The Dravidians were the original inhabitants of India whom the invading Aryans supposedly conquered, dominated and drove to the south. This idea has been to turn the people of southern India against the people of northern India, as if the darker-skinned southerners were a different race. European thinkers of that time believed in a racial theory of man that was based on colour alone. They saw themselves as belonging to a superior 'white' or Caucasian race.

A darker-skinned person in southern India

> Research the meaning of 'Aryan People' on the web!

> Carefully study the features of the people in these photographs. Then identify the similarities between each person's features that indicate they belong to the same ethnic group.

Aryan and Dravidian – One People

The idea of Aryan and Dravidian races is the product of unscientific, culturally biased form of thinking that saw races in terms of colour. There are scientifically speaking, no such things as Aryan or Dravidian races. The three primary races are the Caucasian, the Asian and the black African. Both the Aryans and Dravidians are related branches of the Caucasian race. The difference between the so-called Aryans of the north of India and Dravidians of the south of India is not a racial division. Biologically both the northern and southern Indians are of the same Caucasian race, only when closer to the equator does the skin become darker, due to the creation of melanin, a vitamin needed to combat the effects of ultraviolet light (see page 3). This leads to lighter-skinned people living in the north and darker-skinned people living in the south of the country. The fact that both groups spoke different languages was a cultural fact rather than anything else. In fact there are over seventeen different languages with 900 dialects spoken in India.
(Adapted from *Aryan/Dravidian Controversy* by David Frawley ... research this on the web).

While Indian people may differ in colour due to the effects of the sun's rays, their facial characteristics are Caucasian.

Class activity
1. Explain the historical factors in India that led to racial discrimination based on skin colour alone.
2. Explain the part played directly or indirectly by religions in racial discrimination in India.
3. Get one student to print off the article by David Frawley from which the article printed here was sourced. Then explain the original theory of different races in India.
4. Which are the primary races?
5. Where did the Aryans come from?
6. Who were the Dravidians?

TEST YOURSELF AT
my-etest.com

CHAPTER 6
THE IMPACT OF COLONISATION AND MIGRATION ON RACIAL PATTERNS

The British, French, Spanish and Portuguese were the main colonisers in America and Africa. The descendants of these Europeans are found in those areas that were colonised by them. In some cases descendants of native peoples from these colonies are found in the countries of the colonial powers.

Asylum seekers and refugees
See 'Migration Policies in the European Union and Ireland' in *Our Dynamic World 3*, Chapter 6.

RACIAL GROUPS IN NORTH AND SOUTH AMERICA

The **Portuguese**, French, **Spanish** and British were the main colonists in the Americas. Many people from each of these countries emigrated to these colonies to claim free land and avail of the chance of a better quality of life than they had at home. So Caucasians are the most dominant racial group in these regions. However, the British, French and Portuguese brought **black slaves** from west Africa to work on their plantations in these colonies and so we find a sizeable population of the Afro-American racial group in those areas that were colonised during the time of the slave trade. These regions include Brazil, the Caribbean Islands and the eastern edge of the United States.

See also 'Ireland's immigration policy' in *Our Dynamic World 3*, Chapter 6.

United States

The most important stream of international migrants in the region, in recent times, has been from Mexico and Central America to the United States. Jobs, higher wages and better living conditions have been the major pull factors. Hispanics, already close to 30 per cent of the population of Texas, will most likely be the largest minority in the United States within the next ten years.

Nationality or ethnicity is an important social and political issue in America. The distribution pattern and percentage of population of its ethnic groups has always been influenced by immigration. Roughly 1 million immigrants enter the United States each year. The source areas, however, have changed dramatically over the past forty years. During the 1950s, just over 50 per cent came from Europe, 25 per cent from Central and South America and 15 per cent from Canada. Today 37 per cent come from Asia, another 38 per cent from Central and South America, and about 19 per cent from Europe and Canada. These immigrant percentages together with existing ethnic groups and associated fertility rates are creating a distribution pattern where **American people are choosing to live in distinct regions with others exactly like themselves**. This is causing a **regionalisation of distinct groups** within the United States.

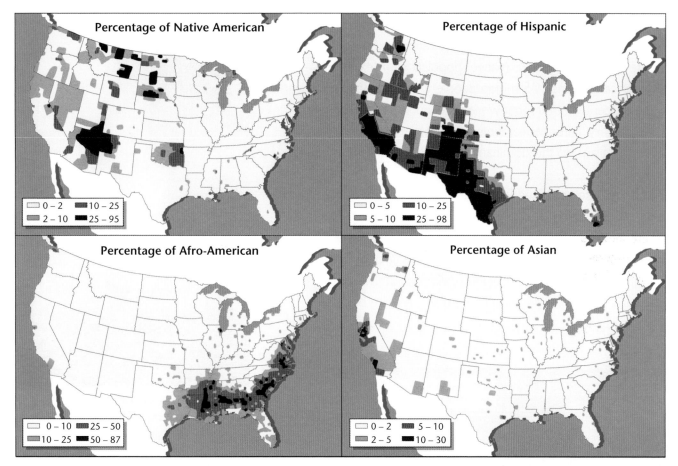

Fig. 6.1 Distribution of ethnic groups in America

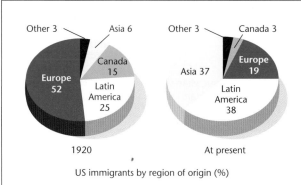

US immigrants by region of origin (%)

Fig. 6.2 Perceived economic opportunity, war, and immigration policy all contribute to fluctuating levels in the flow of migrants.

Remember the key ideas from your Junior Certificate that most migrants settle in those regions nearest to where they came from originally.

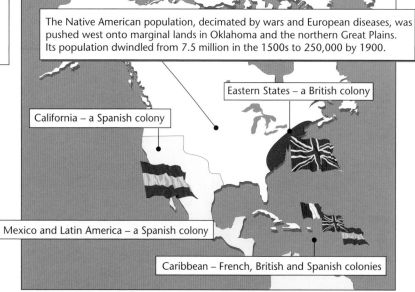

The Native American population, decimated by wars and European diseases, was pushed west onto marginal lands in Oklahoma and the northern Great Plains. Its population dwindled from 7.5 million in the 1500s to 250,000 by 1900.

Eastern States – a British colony

California – a Spanish colony

Mexico and Latin America – a Spanish colony

Caribbean – French, British and Spanish colonies

Fig. 6.3 Some colonies that influenced racial distribution patterns in the United States.

Activities

Carefully examine Fig. 6.1.

1. Explain why:
   (a) Most Native Americans live in upland areas of the west
   (b) Most Hispanics live in the south west
   (c) Most Afro-Americans live in the south west and east
   (d) Most Asians live in the west.
2. What conclusions can be drawn from Fig. 6.2?

21

Latin America

The European colonists brought disease, starvation and war to Latin America, devastating indigenous (native) populations. Mexico and Central America contained 25 million people when the Spanish arrived early in the sixteenth century, but were reduced to 1.1 million by the end of that century. Later movements added other Europeans, mainly Germans and Italians, to the dominant classes, especially in Argentina and Brazil.

The Portuguese colonised Brazil and introduced black slaves from Africa to work on their cotton, sugar and coffee plantations. The descendants of these slaves live along Brazil's east coast today. So Afro-Americans and Caucasians are the dominant ethnic groups in Brazil.

The Spanish colonised most of the remainder of the continent. So Caucasians and Native Americans (Amerindians) are the dominant groups in this region.

Forest destruction is forcing indigenous American Indians out of their traditional homelands and into cities.

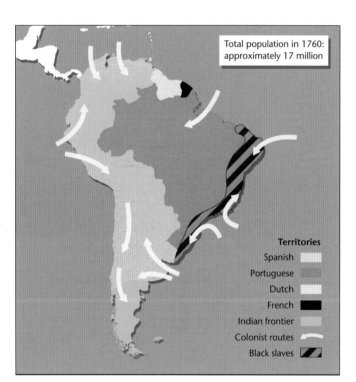

Total population in 1760: approximately 17 million

Territories
Spanish
Portuguese
Dutch
French
Indian frontier
Colonist routes
Black slaves

Fig. 6.4 Colonial America around 1760

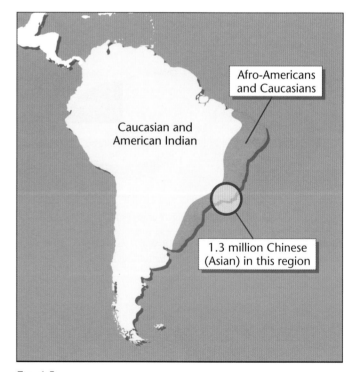

Afro-Americans and Caucasians

Caucasian and American Indian

1.3 million Chinese (Asian) in this region

Fig. 6.5

Class activity
Write two foolscap pages on the influence of colonisation on South America. In your answer refer to:
- at least one conquistador
- the influence on religion
- the influence on language (see page 28)
- the influence on racial groups.

TEST YOURSELF AT
my-etest.com

CHAPTER 7
LANGUAGE AS A
CULTURAL INDICATOR

The development of speech and language has been one of the most fundamental developments of human cultural evolution. It is the means by which people can express themselves and communicate with others. It is also the chief means by which one's heritage is passed on from one generation to the next. **A common language acts as a powerful cementing factor in a social group. It welds the people into a community and develops mutual understanding, so it is important in creating nationality.** Conversely, the existence of different languages, whether between or within states, such as within India, may be an obstacle to understanding, co-operation and unity within that country.

For example, English has become an official language in India to enable communication among the various groups and to avoid recognising one tribal language above others. Differences in language mean differences in culture and are a potential **source of misunderstanding** and **conflict** between nations and ethnic groups. Contact between cultures is increasingly common in our world economy, and this causes languages to be in constant change. Still, great efforts are made by some groups to preserve their linguistic identities.

Case Study: Euskara – the Language of the Basques

The Basque people are very proud of their culture, and their language forms a crucial part of their unique identity. The history of their language has played its part in creating a Basque culture. The language of the Basques is called Euskara. It is spoken by about 520,000 people – about 25 per cent of the Basque people in Spain. It is one of the oldest living languages and is not known to be related to any other language, so it is not Indo-European. It is believed that it was spoken in the Basque region in Neolithic or Stone Age times. The first written texts in Basque date from the tenth century.

Language and communication is the key to understanding cultures and to creating peace and harmony in a society.

Things have not been easy for the Basque language. Besides competing with Spanish and French, Basque was a forbidden language after the Spanish Civil War in the 1930s during the reign of the dictator General Franco. Children had to study in unfamiliar Spanish in school and were punished if they spoke Basque, their native tongue. However, Basque schools called 'iskastolas' started at that time in defiance of this policy. This helped the Basque language to be taught in state schools.

Because there were many dialects of Basque, steps were taken in 1964 to create a unified Basque language.

Bilingual signposts along the Mexican border with the USA reflect the huge Hispanic population in this area.

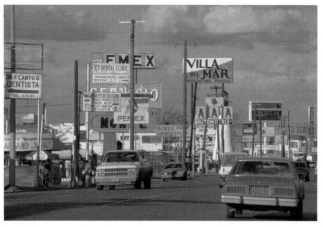

The importance of language as a cultural identifier involves language issues in numerous political conflicts, ranging from regional self-government (such as in the Catalan region in north-east Spain) and the Basque region of northern Spain to the selection of languages in which school classes should be taught.

In many Western European countries, as well as in the United States, schools are under increasing pressure to find strategies to address the special needs of students whose home-language is not the language used in school.

In the United States, which has as yet no official language, numerous language-based political issues have arisen in recent years. The choice of which language(s) to use in primary schools has become a major issue as the number of Spanish-speaking residents has increased by about half a million per year for the past twenty years. Some other schools have 'Black English Vernacular' called **Ebonics**, as a separate language and so demand bilingual education. Several other groups, such as 'English First' and 'English Only' oppose the use of other languages and seek to have laws passed to establish English as the sole official language of the United States.

As a symbol of their culture, members of an ethnic group may seek to protect their language from being overwhelmed by the language of the dominant society. So in Chinatowns in cities, Chinese is the favoured language as it forms part of the identity of the majority of people within that ghetto area. Its street signs and shop fronts all add to its character as a cultural region.

In some urban regions, cultural groups retain their traditional language for dialogue among their own culture.

Class activity
Explain how language can lead to cultural regions within cities.

Foreign students in Ireland use English because it is the most dominant language here.

'Cultural regions' is the general term for areas where some portion of the population shares some degree of cultural identity. Language is clearly evident in such regions through place names. The choice of language on signs is another visible symbol of culture on the landscape. Toponymy, the study of place names can reveal the history of a region and the values of the people, for example, New York in the USA and York in England, New Orleans after Orleans in France.

Criteria to define such regions must be chosen carefully. In some cases it may be convenient to use a single factor, such as language, to define regions such as Gaeltacht areas. In this instance, both the physical and cultural landscapes of the widely separated Gaeltacht regions mostly all lie in the West of Ireland. They have a rugged terrain with small farms, scattered villages, and few public services available locally. A majority of people within these areas all identify with the same language and religion. However, the case of the **English language as a factor in determining culture is useful** only in **its broadest scale** because of the numerous peoples whose primary language is English. English, Irish, Canadians, Americans, Scots, Nigerians, Jamaicans and Indians all speak the English language as their primary tongue. However, they differ greatly in their cultures. For example, Americans and Canadians are often thought by some (including Americans) to share a single culture. However, Canadians have their own specific values, heroes and traditions despite sharing language, religion, technology and other cultural traits with the United States.

Class activity
Is language alone always an exact cultural indicator?

In the 1990s a number of cities in western India were renamed in the regional Gujarati language in response to a Hindu cultural revival: Bombay, for example, is now Mumbai.

See 'Cultural Regions' in *Our Dynamic World 1*.

The West of Ireland has a distinctive cultural character.

French colonies in Africa have French as their primary tongue.

TEST YOURSELF AT
my-etest.com

25

CHAPTER 8
THE ORIGIN AND SPREAD OF LANGUAGES

As with many other questions about human evolution, there is still no consensus about the origins of speech and language. Some scholars have suggested that art and language must be closely interwoven, because they both require the ability to understand abstract ideas and concepts and to share these understandings with others as part of a cultural system. According to this theory, fully developed languages would not have existed before the appearance of art, which first emerged about 40,000 years ago.

The complexity of human language and speech is dependent on a number of brain and body mechanisms found only in our species – *Homo Sapiens*. These include a vocal tract (voice box) that permits a wide range of speech sounds, areas of the brain that control and interpret these sounds, and an efficient memory that can use past experiences as a guide to the future.

Even though thousands of languages are spoken in the world today, populations that share similar cultures and live only a short distance apart may still speak languages that are quite distinct from and not readily understood by neighbouring populations. For example, the inhabitants of New Guinea and neighbouring islands speak approximately 1,000 different languages, or about one-fifth of the world's total.

The first languages were dispersed in a number of ways:

Tourists, migrations and business transactions throughout Europe have led to the introduction of languages such as Italian, French and German into Irish schools.

- The most obvious dispersal was migration. As they spread out across the globe, early peoples carried their languages into uninhabited territory.
- Languages would also have spread as a result of contact between different peoples. For example, the invention and adoption of food production (called the Neolithic Spread) would have encouraged agricultural peoples to migrate into territories occupied by hunter-gatherers, who may then have adopted both the cultivation techniques and language of the immigrants.
- A third form of language dispersal involves the replacement of an existing language by one spoken by a dominant group. The development of complex societies allowed incoming minorities with some form of centralised organisation to dominate larger populations, which in many cases, later adopted the language of the elite. For example, the adoption of the Chinese language family in southern China in historical times occurred as a result of the military

expansion of the Chinese Empire. Just as many countries, including Ireland, adopted English as a consequence of the military expansion of the British Empire.

THE MAJOR LANGUAGE FAMILIES

Italian migration into the United States led to large Italian-speaking communities in many US cities.

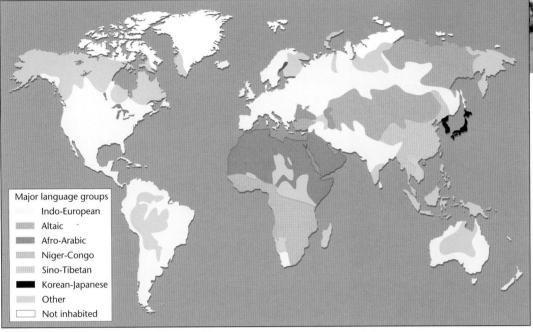

Major language groups
- Indo-European
- Altaic
- Afro-Arabic
- Niger-Congo
- Sino-Tibetan
- Korean-Japanese
- Other
- Not inhabited

Fig. 8.1 The major languages of the world.

Most Indian people in southern Asia speak a language that is related to the Indo-European tongue.

Activity

Identify the language that is spoken in the following areas:
(a) North Africa and Arabia
(b) India
(c) Brazil
(d) United States
(e) Australia
Use two examples of the above and explain why those languages are spoken in these areas.

Similarities exist between languages used in different parts of the world, which suggest that they developed from a common source or tongue. Scholars group such languages into language groups, or language families, on the basis of similarities in vocabulary, sound systems and grammar. All members of each language family are related. English, for example, is part of the Indo-European family and so are Italian and Spanish.

Indo-European Family

The Indo-European family is the most important language family. About half the world's population speak languages from this family. Most of the nations that gave rise to Western civilisation speak Indo-European languages. No-one knows where the parent Indo-European language was first spoken. It probably began in the area south of the Baltic Sea.

Its speakers migrated to various regions and the language changed along the way. They now live in other regions such as North and South America, across Russia to the Pacific Ocean and southern Asia including Iran, Iraq and Pakistan and northern India as well as Malaysia and Australia. This language spread mainly through conquest and colonisation.

In North America, Britain and France took control of the land, while in Central and South America the Spanish and Portuguese introduced the Portuguese language (Brazil) and the Spanish language from Mexico southwards to Argentina and Chile. It is important to note that the northern half of India speaks Indo-European while the southern half speaks Dravidian. Indo-European was brought to northern India by groups of migrants that wandered eastwards from central Europe. The Indo-European family has eight living branches. They are:

Many words in German and English originate from a common tongue.

- Germanic – which includes English, German, Dutch Flemish, and the Scandinavian tongues – Danish, Icelandic, Norwegian and Swedish
- Romance, or Latin-Romance – which includes French, Spanish, Portuguese Italian and Romanian
- Balto-Slavic – which includes Russian, Ukrainian, Polish, Czech, Slovak, Serbo-Croatian, Slovenian, Bulgarian, Lithuanian and Latvian
- Indo-Iranian – which includes Hindustani, Bengali, Persian and Pashto
- Greek
- Celtic including Irish, Scots Gaelic, Welsh and Breton
- Albanian
- Armenian

Many simple, basic words are similar in Indo-European languages. For example, the English word mother is *meter* in Greek, *mater* in Latin, *madre* in Spanish, *mutter* in German and *mat* in Russian.

Case Study: The Languages of India

In *Our Developing World 1* you learned that most of the languages of India came from four language families: Indo-European, Dravidian, Mon Khmer and Sino-Tibetan. Most of northern and central India uses Indo-European languages. The most important of these languages is Hindi, which is spoken by about 25 per cent of the Indian population. The Dravidian languages dominate in the south of the country.

Indo-European languages were introduced to northern and central India by nomadic tribes. Initially

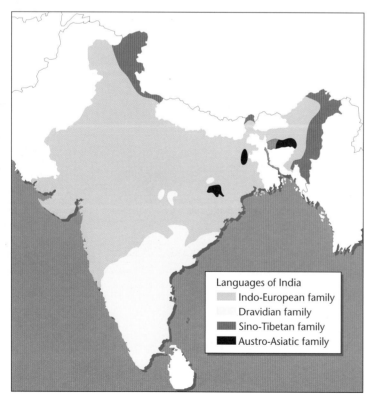

Languages of India
- Indo-European family
- Dravidian family
- Sino-Tibetan family
- Austro-Asiatic family

Fig. 8.2

it was believed that these nomads fought great battles with native Indians and drove them southwards to create this Dravidian and Indo-European language divide as is clearly seen on the map, Fig. 8.2. Today however, linguists believe that Indo-European influences were introduced gradually by these nomadic groups over a long period of time and that the process was much slower and without the violence and racial divisions that were believed to exist up until recently.

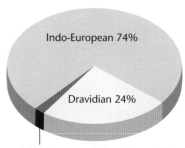

Indo-European 74%

Dravidian 24%

Mon Khmer and Sino-Tibetan 2%

Fig. 8.3

See 'Languages' in *Our Dynamic World 1*, Chapter 21, India. This is a link to your case studies.

Punjabi is the language spoken by the Sikhs who are the majority cultural group in the Punjab, a state in northern India.

Sino-Tibetan Family

The Sino-Tibetan language family is second in importance with over one billion speakers. This family includes Chinese with its many dialects, as well as Thai, Burmese and Tibetan. These languages are the leading languages of East Asia. The Sino-Tibetan or Chinese languages consist of one-syllable words. Speakers show the different meanings of otherwise identical words by changing their tone of voice. This language is one of the oldest living languages and has been spoken since about 2000 BC. Its many dialects differ enough in pronunciation to be considered foreign languages. China has suffered many invasions in the past and has seen many empires come and go. Each of these has had an effect on language and dialect. It has also always been heavily populated and during some of the dynasties many Chinese migrated southwards in search of better land and living conditions. Mountain ranges run north/south to south-east Asia and so valleys provided corridors of migration for many hundreds of thousands of people. These migrations influenced language in agricultural regions to the south such as Thailand and Myanmar (Burma).

The Chinatown sections of Western cities have a distinctive character with their bright neon language signs and Oriental-style building designs. (See 'Ghettos' in chapter 17 of *Our Dynamic World 3*.)

The Arabic language and Islamic faith unites people across north Africa and in Arabian countries creating a distinctive cultural region.

Arabic-Semitic Family

The Arabic-Semitic language family, which includes Hebrew and Arabic, is concentrated in north and north-east Africa, the Middle East and the Arabian Peninsula. It includes countries such as Morocco, Algeria, Tunisia and Egypt. The spread of the Muslim faith across north Africa brought the Arabic language to this region and it is the official language of these countries. In addition, the gold and salt trades used the caravan routes that crossed the Sahara, this created dialogue and helped the spread of Arabic (see Islam, page 38).

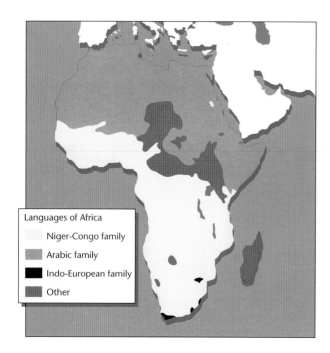

Languages of Africa

☐ Niger-Congo family

☐ Arabic family

■ Indo-European family

☐ Other

Fig. 8.4 Africa has many languages especially in areas south of the Sahara Desert.

Swahili developed as a 'pidgin' language due to contact between African and Arab traders along the East African coast.

The Ural and Altaic Family

The Ural and Altaic language family includes Finnish, Hungarian, Turkish, Mongol, Manchu and most of the languages spoken in the Asian part of Russia.

Niger-Congo Family

The Niger-Congo language family group is also called Bantu. The language is used in an area stretching from the Sudan in the north to South Africa in the south and extending across the entire width of Africa to include The Democratic Republic of Congo, Somalia, Mozambique and Tanzania. It includes many tribal languages including Swahili, which developed as a pidgin language for trading purposes between Arab and African traders. This language group probably originated in what is now Cameroon.

At about the time of Christ the Bantu began one of the greatest migrations in history. These people were farmers who knew how to make iron tools and weapons and brought the knowledge of iron-making to much of Africa, just as the Celts brought the knowledge of iron-making and the Celtic language from Europe to Britain and Ireland. The migration began gradually with small groups splitting off and moving to new areas where they are still located today.

Japanese and Korean Family

The Japanese and Korean language family is largely limited to Japan, North Korea and South Korea.

Dravidian Family

The Dravidian language family is located in southern India and Sri Lanka. It consists of Tamil, Telugu and other languages.

Class activity

1. Carefully study the language distribution map of India, Fig. 8.2, page 28. Then explain why skin colour and language provided useful tools in the creation of ethnic conflict and discrimination in India.
2. Explain how a language of the Sino-Tibetan family helps create cultural regions within American and some European cities.
3. Explain how the recent spread of new languages to Ireland is helping to create cultural areas in Dublin. (Hint: Liberties region.)

TEST YOURSELF AT
my-etest.com

CHAPTER 9
THE INFLUENCE OF
MASS MEDIA ON LANGUAGE

Some languages spread faster than others. In the past this may have been due to colonisation and migration. However, some languages, such as English, are promoted indirectly, but with increasing success, by the influence of television and the internet. News is one of the foundation stones of broadcasting and quality news programmes have major viewing appeal.

Programmes such as Sky News and CNN, with their ability to transmit images and news information as it happens, have increased the influence of the English language throughout the world. Such satellite world news coverage enters peoples' homes on a daily basis so increasing the influence of English.

Does film influence the spread of language? Explain.

Modern technology, such as television and radio, helps the spread of dominant languages.

The advance in communications systems has led to increased contact with other cultures. How can this negatively effect some languages? Explain.

Sami is a native language of northern Europe that is in danger of extinction.

Has TG4 helped in the promotion of the Irish language? Explain.

Activity
Suggest two other ways in which English has become a threatening influence to other languages. In one instance, refer to the influence of film as a threat.

TEST YOURSELF AT
my-etest.com

CHAPTER 10
POLICIES FOR SURVIVAL OF MINORITY LANGUAGES

It is believed that **diversity is the cornerstone of innovative development within the European Union (EU).** It is argued that language plays a central role in diversity, so attention must be given to maintaining this existing pool of variety within the EU. In various parts of EU countries, indeed in various parts of non-EU countries, there are substantial numbers of people who are citizens of a state who speak a different language to that of the language spoken by the majority of the state's population. It is estimated that as many as 40 million citizens of the EU regularly use a regional or minority language that has been passed on from generation to generation, generally in addition to the official language or languages of that state. These languages are not those of immigrants or dialects of official languages but are recognised by the **European Charter for Regional or Minority Languages**.

Language plays a very important role in creating cultural identity. La Sardana, Catalunya's national dance, is performed every week on Plaça de la Seu, in Barcelona.

This definition covers a wide variety of languages and an equally wide variety of social, political and language situations. Catalan, for example, is spoken by some 7 million people in north-east Spain, south-west France and the town of Alghero in Sardinia. Most Catalan speakers live in the self-governing communities of north-east Spain where it is spoken by the majority of the population and has official status alongside Spanish.

Sami, on the other hand, is a family of languages spoken by indigenous (native) peoples in northern Finland, Sweden, Norway and the Kola Peninsula of Russia, some members of which have only a few hundred speakers and are in real danger of extinction.

Additional examples include Irish and Luxembourgish, which despite their official status as national languages in their own countries, bear many of the characteristics of regional and minority languages. In total, over sixty indigenous regional and minority language communities can be identified. Some of these share many common factors that bring them together. These include, for instance, the Basque and Catalan speaking communities of France and Spain that have part of their communities in each country. Others have traditional, cultural and historical ties such as the Celtic language communities of France, Ireland, Scotland and Wales. All of these minority language groups, however, share a deep interest in the survival and continued development of their languages and cultures and the importance of their contribution towards the diversity of cultures within the EU.

Activity

One could ask why bother preserving these minority languages that are now struggling to survive? Well, one could also ask why bother preserving most languages. Let's all use English and life might be simpler ... maybe it would, but would it be better? Discuss.

GAELTACHT REGIONS

In *Our Dynamic World 1* you studied the Gaeltacht areas that are scattered along the western and southern coasts of Ireland from Donegal to Waterford. You also learnt that their total populations amounted to 86,000 people and of these over 61,000 of them over the age of three years spoke Irish. The Gaeltacht regions are the heartland of Gaelic language and culture. However, there are great changes in the boundaries of the Gaeltacht since it was first established. The present Gaeltacht, where Irish is the majority language, is much reduced in area and is today confined to relatively small isolated pockets mainly in the peninsulas of the west coast of Ireland. Yet their presence forms an integral part of Ireland as a nation and their special importance is supported by government grants, pay allowances and other financial incentives (see *Our Dynamic World 1*, Chapter 25).

The Irish language is promoted by radio and TV programmes. Would you consider this a successful way of promoting Irish?

Initially there were two categories of Gaeltacht regions:

(a) In Fior Gaeltacht districts over 8 per cent of the population spoke Irish in their everyday life.

(b) In a Breac Gaeltacht district between 25 and 79 per cent of the population spoke Irish.

Using these criteria the commission that was established in 1925 was able to identify and create distinctive cultural regions based on the Irish language. Today in the Republic of Ireland there are 1.5 million people who claim to have some ability to speak and understand Irish. This totals over 41 per cent of the population of the state and it is over three times the number of people who claimed this ability in 1926. This increase reflects the continued efforts of government and voluntary bodies who promote the Irish language.

Annual Feiseanna, such as Fleadh Cheoil na hEireann, promote Irish culture and traditions.

Initiatives for the Survival of the Irish Language

Some initiatives are government sponsored while others are voluntary. Some of these initiatives include:

- Festivals that promote the language through art exhibitions and music
- An audio-visual industry that promotes Irish culture within the Gaeltacht and throughout Ireland. These influences include:
  (a) Radio na Gaeltachta
  (b) The TV station TG4
- Local radio stations such as Leirithe Lunasa Teo in Corca Dhuibhne and Nemeton Teo in An Rinn
- Irish language schools, na Gaelscoilanna

Class activity

1. Do you think that Gaeltacht areas are distinctive cultural regions? Why? In your answer refer to
   - language
   - location
   - landscape.

2. Write as much as you can on any two initiatives for the survival of the Irish language. Say how successful you think each has been.

- Summer colleges in the Gaeltacht areas. These are also a welcome and vital source of income for families who provide accommodation and food for the students, as well as bringing the students in direct contact with Gaeltacht families.

Supports for Survival

- Respect for linguistic and cultural diversity is one of the cornerstones of the EU. This ideal is now enshrined in **Article 22 of the European Charter of Fundamental Rights**, which states 'The **Union respects cultural, religious and linguistic diversity**'.
- The European Bureau of Lesser-Used Languages (EBLUL), is an organisation at the European Headquarters in Brussels. It works on behalf of those in the EU who speak minority languages. It creates and promotes policies that support these languages that are under threat from extinction. As mentioned already these languages may be like rare plants that inhabit just a few mountain valleys. For example, Ladin is a language that exists in the Dolomite Mountain region of northern Italy and the Alps in eastern Switzerland. There are small Italian-speaking communities in Slovenia and Croatia, and Polish-speaking communities in the Czech Republic. All these minority languages are in danger of being swallowed up by the majority language in those countries.
- The EU gives financial support to the EBLUL and its information network.
- It also offers funding for practical initiatives aimed at protecting and promoting regional and minority languages.
- International conferences are held at regular intervals to identify ways to improve the situations of minority languages that are under threat. These are organised by the FEL, the Foundation for Endangered Languages.

> Find out the names of some of the festivals that promote the Irish language and culture and write a brief note about these activities and events.

> Some county development plans support the Gaeltacht areas by demanding that place names are written in both Gaelic and English.

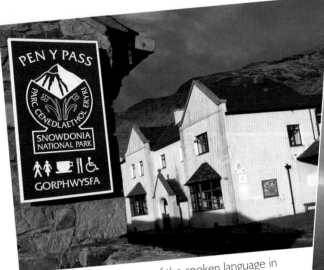

Signposts are an indication of the spoken language in a region. Is it important that some signposts should be bilingual?

Ladin is a minority language spoken in some valley regions in the Austrian mountains.

Class activity

1. Explain the importance of the EBLUL in helping minority languages within the EU.
2. Explain how the survival of the Basque minority language plays its part in creating a cultural region within northern Spain. (See pages 68-69.)

TEST YOURSELF AT
my-etest.com

CHAPTER 11
RELIGION AS A CULTURAL INDICATOR

Religion, like language, can be a defining component of a cultural identity and one that provides the basis for the choice of clothing, food, tools and occupation.

As a social system based on the concept of a divine being, or god, and involving beliefs, values and behaviours, religion organises many aspects of culture.

Religion changes landscapes through the construction of religious buildings, such as churches. Mosques with their minarets (towers) are visibly different from churches and contribute to the difference between Muslim and Christian landscapes. The absence of particular types of building, such as bars and pig farms from Muslim communities, occurs because alcohol and pork are taboo in Islam.

The choice of clothing, such as the concealing chador worn by Muslim women, and headwear, such as the turbans worn by Sikh men and their long beards, are personal signs of those religions. Shared beliefs and values establish strong group identification and because groups can also be linked to specific areas, certain patterns of different religions result.

Attitudes to women, birth control and materialism also can be associated with patterns relating to certain religions.

While most religions involve the worship of some god, or gods, supreme beings play a minor role in some faiths, such as Buddhism. Nor do all religions have practices, core doctrines or moral codes that are common to every follower.

The great majority of the world's religions evolved among particular peoples who had no interest in attracting converts. Few tribal peoples, for example, would attempt to persuade their neighbours to adopt their religious beliefs and practices. Similarly some prominent religions such as Hinduism and Judaism make no effort to seek converts.

However, this is not always the case. Religion is often the cause of great social conflict, particularly when two proselytising religions are in competition. Even within religions that have a core doctrine, comparatively minor differences of faith or practice can cause bitter divisions, such as between Catholic and Protestant communities in Northern Ireland. Frequently, religious conflicts are aggravated by historical factors and by the extent to which religious divisions are influenced by other divisions, such as language, ethnicity and class.

Sikhs' clothing is culturally distinctive.

Muslim women wear a chador as part of their culture.

Class activity
1. Explain how religion plays its part in creating different cultural groups in Northern Ireland.
2. Explain the part played by religion in creating the Islamic cultural region throughout North Africa and the Middle East.

TEST YOURSELF AT
my-etest.com

Jewish people regard Jerusalem as their holy city.

CHAPTER 12
THE DISTRIBUTION OF THE WORLD'S MAJOR RELIGIONS

PATTERNS OF RELIGIOUS GROUPS

Religious groups tend to be concentrated in regions. The global distribution of these regions reflects past migrations of peoples and the spread of the religions. Religions began in localised areas, such as Christianity in the Holy Land and Islam in Mecca, Saudi Arabia, and then expand outward due to the influence of missionaries and migrations.

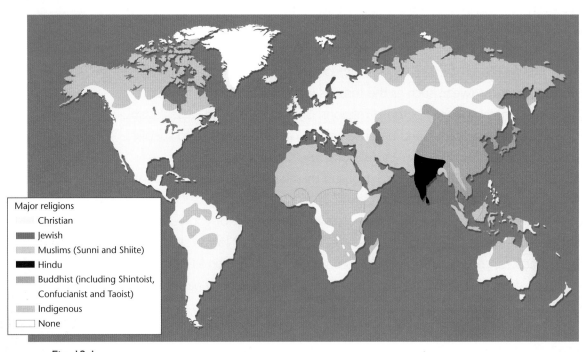

Major religions
- Christian
- Jewish
- Muslims (Sunni and Shiite)
- Hindu
- Buddhist (including Shintoist, Confucianist and Taoist)
- Indigenous
- None

Fig. 12.1

Which religions cover
- The largest area?
- The second largest area?
- Why are some regions listed as having no religion (none)?

Activities
Carefully examine the map showing the distribution of the major religions of the world and Fig. 8.1, page 27, of the major languages of the world. Then do the following:
1. Identify three regions where similarities exist between their distributions
2. Briefly account for these similarities.

Judaism

Judaism was originally the tribal religion of a people who traced their past back to Abraham. Abraham is said to have migrated with his followers from the city of Ur in Mesopotamia (now Iraq) to Canaan in Palestine in the eastern Mediterranean obeying a command of God. The Bible tells us that God promised the land to Abraham and his heirs. Two of Abraham's many sons are particularly remembered. Ishmael became the founder of some Arab tribes. While Isaac, who was Abraham's true heir, became the ancestor of the Israelite people. Isaac's descendants moved to Egypt where they were held in slavery until Moses led them to the promised land across the Red Sea and back to Palestine in about 1200 BC.

Jews, who later migrated throughout the world, thought of Palestine as their spiritual birthplace because their religion developed there. Although Judaism has a comparatively small number of believers, around 14 million, it is important both for its role in the origins of Christianity and Islam, and for its continuing influence on cultural and political events in the Middle East.

Israel was founded to provide a secure homeland for the world's Jews. Since 1948 Jews have travelled from other countries to Israel. Many fled their own lands because of persecution. Israeli law provides that any Jew from anywhere in the world has the right to settle in Israel. In 1970, the law was amended to grant Israeli nationality to the wife of any immigrant Jew, to his descendants for two generations and to the wives of those descendants, whether or not they are Jewish. According to Judaism, a Jew is a person who has a Jewish mother or who has converted to Judaism.

Fig. 12.2 Israel was created to provide a homeland for the Jewish people.

Christianity

Christianity is the largest religious group with over 33 per cent of the world's population as believers. Christianity originated as a movement within Judaism. Fundamental to its doctrine is the belief that Jesus Christ was the Messiah prophesied in the Old Testament. Jesus began his career in Palestine. He travelled around the country with a group of twelve chosen disciples. The Jewish leaders at the time did not approve of his claim that he was the Messiah. The Roman authorities that controlled Palestine felt that Jesus' claim to be 'king' of the Jews amounted to treason. They feared that he meant to lead an uprising against Roman rule in Palestine. So, he was tried, condemned to death and crucified. According to Christian belief, Jesus Christ rose from the dead and appeared to his disciples before ascending to Heaven.

Many cathedrals have Gothic style architecture with pointed arches in windows and doors.

Christianity spread rapidly due to the work of St Paul and other evangelists. The Romans persecuted the Christians for many years until Emperor Constantine granted them freedom of religion. Through the Edict of Milan in AD 313 Christianity became the

St Peter's Basilica in Rome is the centre of the Christian world.

official religion of the Roman Empire. Christianity continued to spread after the fall of the Roman Empire in the fifth century, reaching most of Europe by AD 1000.

During Medieval times the Church strongly influenced political and intellectual life in Europe. It developed great wealth and power and Christianity bound almost all of Europe in a single faith. The rulers of Spain and Portugal were Christians and were the main cause of spreading the Christian faith to the Americas. During the fifteenth and sixteenth centuries in particular, the Christian faith was spread to North and South America by the actions of the Conquistadors, Cortes, Pizzaro and Christopher Columbus.

Canada was colonised by the French and the British, while the USA was mainly British up to the eighteenth century. During the nineteenth century, mass migration from Europe took place. Irish, Italians, Norwegians and Scots flocked to America. In the nineteenth and twentieth centuries the British colonised Australia and the Jesuits were influential in carrying Christianity to China. Christianity had spread throughout Russia before the Russian Revolution against the Czar Nicholas.

> Can you identify some cultural symbols of everyday life of people of the Christian faith?

Islam

Islam is the name given to the religion preached by the Prophet Mohammed in the seventh century. Mohammed was an Arab who was born in Mecca about 570. He believed he had been sent to warn and guide his people and to call them to worship God, Allah. Mohammed preached that there is only one god and that he, Mohammed, was god's messenger. Those who believe in this faith are called Muslims. Muslim comes from the Arabic word Muslim, meaning one who submits (to god). Islam is Arabic for submission.

Fig. 12.3

Activity
Carefully examine the flow chart showing the spread of Islam. Then answer the following:
1. Which European countries were affected by the spread of Islam?
2. Identify two ways this migration has affected the culture and life of people in any two of these European countries.

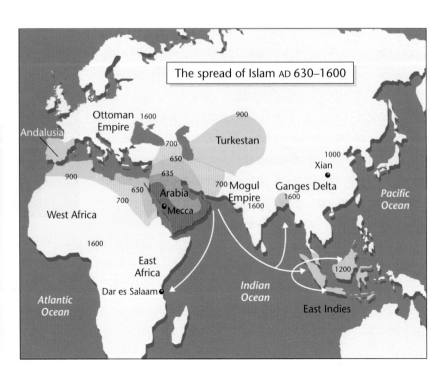

Islam sprang from the same root as Judaism and Christianity. When Mohammed founded Islam in the seventh century, he had contact with both Jewish and Christian communities. He came to regard the Jewish-Christian prophets including Christ, as prophets of Islam. After receiving revelations about the worship of one god, Allah, Mohammed began to preach against the polytheistic (the doctrine of more than one god) practices of Mecca at that time. Persecution then forced him and his followers, called Muslims, to flee to Medina. This migration which took place in AD 622 marks the beginning of the Muslim calendar. In AD 630 Mohammed and his followers returned to Mecca and captured the city. They destroyed all the idols in the pagan temple and turned the area around it into a mosque. The Meccans then accepted Islam and Mohammed as their prophet. Mecca and Medina became the sacred cities of Islam.

The spread of Islam throughout the Middle East and north Africa began with conquests launched from Mecca and Medina. After Mohammed died in AD 632, the new Caliph or Muslim ruler and his successors waged holy war, called *Jihad*. Within a hundred years they had built an empire across the **hot desert**

Muslims in Arab nations wear distinctive clothing.

lands that stretched from northern Spain and north-west Africa to India. The Muslims threatened Western Europe until Charles Martel defeated them at the Battle of Tours in 732. A consequence of this colonisation process can be seen in the influence of the Moors in Spain and by the presence of large numbers of Muslim people in countries that make up former Yugoslavia.

'Moors' is the name given to Arabs who invaded Spain from north Africa.

The Arab conquerors taught the inhabitants of their captured lands their Arabic language and their Islamic faith. The **Arabic language eventually replaced the native languages** in most of these regions and Arabic became the language of the Muslim culture. However, in countries east of the Arabian peninsula, such as in Iran and in Iraq, it is the Indo-European languages that are spoken, even though they practise Islam.

Islam has **two major branches**, **Sunni** and **Shiite**. This separation occurred during the seventh century over leadership of the religion. Sunnis make up about 84 per cent of all Muslims and dominate the Arabian peninsula, northern Africa, and most Muslim countries around the world. Shiites are the majority of the population in Iran, which is about 90 per cent Shiite, and in Iraq, which is some 60 to 65 per cent Shiite. So the Indo-European speaking Shiites mainly live east of Arabia, while the Arabic speaking Sunnis live west of the Arabian peninsula.

Muslims on Manger Square in Bethlehem face east towards Mecca to pray.

Activities
1. From which city and state did Islam spread?
2. When did Islam reach India and Pakistan?
3. When did Islam reach north-west Africa?
4. Who was the conquering group that brought Islam to south-eastern Europe? When did this occur?
5. Explain one example of conflict in the twentieth century that arose as a result of migration/ religious influence.

Millions of Hindus gather here at the steps in Varanasi to wash in the sacred River Ganges.

Hinduism

Hinduism is mostly confined to the Indian sub-continent and parts of south-east Asia, such as Malaysia and Indonesia, mainly because of its non-missionary nature. Hinduism has its roots in the religion of Indo-European peoples who migrated into India some thousands of years ago. The sacred texts of Hinduism are the Vedas, which explore the place of human beings, and the roles played by various gods, in the functioning of the universe. Hindus are monotheists. They believe in one high god, Brahman, the Absolute. Hinduism may be divided into three branches or sects each with its own view of the nature and name of the high god, Visnu, Shiva or Shakti.

Families, by long tradition, support one branch or another. All branches are to be found in every part of India. The three sects continue together more or less in harmony. Educated Hindus believe that the three gods are merely differing ways of looking at the same high god.

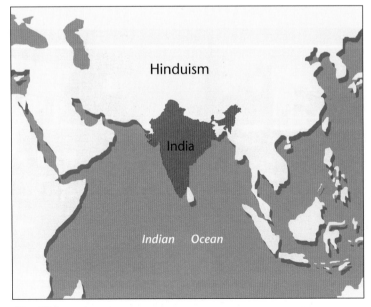

Fig. 12.4

Class activity
Read the extract on the Ganges and then do the following.
1. Identify the centre of the Hindu faith.
2. Identify the Hinduism's sacred river.
3. Explain why Hindus bathe in the Ganges.
4. Explain how some Christian traditions and beliefs are held in common with the Hindu faith.
5. Explain two main causes of pollution in the River Ganges.
6. Explain why many Hindu temples are falling into decay.
7. To which area of India is the term 'ghat' applied? Explain why its name may reflect its origin.

Stand on the banks of the Ganges River in Varanasi, Hinduism's holiest city, and you will see people bathing in the holy water, drinking it, and praying as they stand in it – while the city's sewage flows into it nearby, and the partially cremated corpses of people and animals float past. It is one of the world's most compelling – and disturbing – sights.

The Ganges (*Ganga* as the Indians call it) is Hinduism's sacred river. Tradition has it, the river's water is immaculate, and no amount of human (or other) waste can pollute it. On the contrary: just touching the water can wash away a believer's sins.

At Varanasi, Allahabad, and other cities and towns along the Ganges, the riverbanks are lined with Hindu temples, decaying ornate palaces, and dozens of wide stone staircases called *ghats*. These stepped platforms lead down to the water, enabling thousands of bathers to enter the river. They come from the city and from afar, many of them pilgrims in need of the healing and spiritual powers of the water. It is estimated that more than a million people enter the river somewhere along its 1,600-mile (2,800-km) course every day. During religious festivals, the number may be ten times as large.

By any standards, the Ganges is one of the world's most severely polluted streams, and thousands among those who enter it become ill with diarrhoea or other diseases; many die. (From *Geography Reams and Regions*)

Buddhism is mostly confined to east and south-east Asia.

Buddhism

Buddhism is one of the major religions of the world. It was founded in India. It is an offshoot of Hinduism based on the teachings of **Siddhartha Gautama**. He was born a member of the Hindu priestly caste about 563 BC. Buddhism started near the border of what are now India and Nepal, where Siddhartha was **born, reached enlightenment** and **died**. Lumbini, now in Nepal, and Bodh Gaya and Kusinagara in India are sacred places in this religious region based on these three events.

Missionaries carried Buddhism to regions of eastern Asia such as China and Japan. Different branches of the religion developed and Buddhism also merged with other religions. The number of Buddhists worldwide is consequently uncertain because individuals often practise Buddhism along with cultural Chinese and Japanese religions. Buddhism is dominant in Tibet, now part of China. It is also common in China, Korea, Japan and in parts of south-east Asia such as Vietnam.

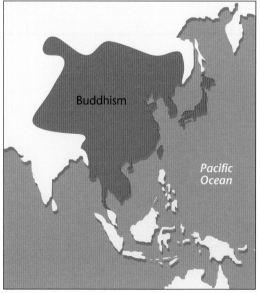

Fig. 12.5

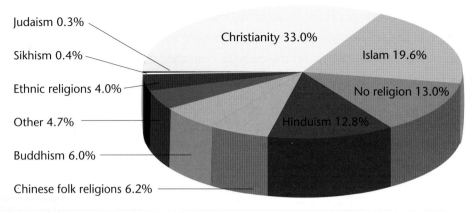

Judaism 0.3%

Sikhism 0.4%

Ethnic religions 4.0%

Other 4.7%

Buddhism 6.0%

Chinese folk religions 6.2%

Christianity 33.0%

Islam 19.6%

No religion 13.0%

Hinduism 12.8%

Fig. 12.6

Activities 1

This pie chart shows the percentages of the world's population belonging to the major religions. Despite their small number, the Jews (0.3 per cent) have had a major influence on history, culture and other religions.

1. List the world's religious groups in rank order.
2. To which language group do most of the world's largest religious group belong? Explain fully.
3. Explain why this religion has spread over such a large number of regions.
4. In which region of the world is Hinduism practised?
5. Which language groups do those that practise Hinduism belong to? Explain fully.
6. Why is it that the Chinese folk religious group make up only 6.2 per cent of the world's population, even though the Chinese number 1.2 billion people?
7. In which cultural region or realm of the world is Islam the dominant religion?
8. Explain why Islam dominates in this area.

Activities 2

1. The success of the spread of Islam and the present-day distribution pattern of the Islamic faith may have been due in part to climatic factors. Discuss.
2. Explain why the Christian faith is practised in areas in Africa that are widely separated from each other.

TEST YOURSELF AT

my-etest.com

CHAPTER 13
THE RELATIONSHIP BETWEEN CHURCH AND STATE

THE IRISH CONSTITUTION

The Irish Constitution of 1937 introduced by Eamonn De Valera recognised the 'special position of the Catholic Church' as the 'religion of the great majority of citizens' (article 44). At the same time the Constitution guaranteed 'freedom of conscience and the free profession and practise of religion' to a list of other religious groups, including the Jewish community who were discriminated against in Germany by Hitler and the Nazi regime at that time. Moreover, this special position of the Catholic Church had been well established in the minds of the Irish nation long before this.

Eamonn de Valera recognised the 'special position of the Catholic Church' as an influencing factor in Irish political affairs.

At the beginning of the eighteenth century a series of harsh laws called 'The Penal Laws' were introduced into Ireland to penalise the vast majority of the Irish people just because they were Roman Catholics. These Penal Laws stated that a Catholic could not hold any office of state, nor stand for parliament, vote, join the army or navy, practise law or buy land. So the association of the Catholic religion with politics, law and land was firmly established in the minds and hearts of the Irish people; it was to dominate Irish society until recent times. Daniel O'Connell's campaign to repeal these laws encouraged this association and he successfully channelled the influence, or in other words the power, of the Catholic Church's bond with the Irish people into politics. He linked them together so firmly that succeeding generations found difficulty in pulling them apart.

Many young people entered religious orders up to the 1970s in Ireland.

Up until the 1970s Irish society was mainly a rural one. The ownership of land played an important part in Eamonn De Valera's image of Ireland and the rural farming communities provided large numbers of young men for the priesthood and religious life. Farming communities and business people could afford, more than others, to send their sons to university (often with state grants), or campaign for political office. This created a religious, farming, professional and political circle of power that continued until recent times.

One of the most controversial issues concerning the power of the Church over state matters that arose during the twentieth century was the 'Mother and Child' scheme. This involved a power struggle between the then Minister for Health, Dr Noel Browne, and the Catholic Church body during the 1950s.

> Research the 'Mother and Child' scheme under Dr Noel Browne.

NORTHERN IRELAND

In 1911, on the island of Ireland, 62 per cent of the members of the Church of Ireland and almost all of the 444,000 Presbyterians lived in the same nine Ulster counties. Political controlling influence was predominantly Presbyterian, industry being a major influence, since it was mostly the Presbyterians who built the docks, the shipyards (the

Regular Orange Order marches displayed the dominance and political power of the Protestant community in Northern Ireland.

largest in the world at that time), and linen mills. Ulster Presbyterianism and the spread of Calvinism from Scotland had its roots in the seventeenth-century plantation of Ulster. The rise of the Orange Order in the nineteenth century by the wealthy landowners and industrialists made this the representative body of the Protestant community.

The Orange Order fostered a sense of community amongst Protestants and institutionalised the instinct of racial superiority over the conquered Catholics. This led to social segregation, especially noticeable in the cities, which led to the ghettos in Belfast and Derry, where Catholics were housed in certain housing estates in one part of a city while Protestants were housed in others. It also led to gerrymandering.

Gerrymandering

After the partition of Ireland, a proportional representation (PR) system of local elections was introduced by the British government to give minorities a fairer say in the electoral system. However, this was seen as a threat to the Ulster state by the unionist government in Northern Ireland and it was abolished in 1922. All local government electoral boundaries were redrawn in such a way that unionist majorities were guaranteed, despite the fact that Catholics formed a majority of the population in many counties. The right to vote for local councils was limited to those who held property and people with several properties had several votes. Since Protestants generally had more property than Catholics, it strengthened Protestant control of Northern Ireland. This system led to widespread corruption and discrimination against Catholics in jobs, housing and other local services; it continued until the 1970s. Civil rights marches, encouraged by successful marches by the black community in the United States, indirectly led to gradual change in Northern Ireland.

Catholic nationalists were forced to march in the 1960s and 1970s to gain civil rights.

Class activity
1. Explain how the influence of the Catholic Church in political affairs evolved over time.
2. Who was Dr Noel Browne? Explain how conflict arose between him and the Church in Ireland during the 1950s.
3. Explain the origin of the Presbyterian faith in Ulster and its influence on politics.

TEST YOURSELF AT
my-etest.com

CHAPTER 14
RELIGIOUS CONFLICT

Members of different religions live side by side without problems in many areas of the world, but religious conflict can arise when different religious communities come into contact. Some conflicts arise over political and economic opportunities while others may occur over beliefs and values.

The following case studies look at some disputes that have risen as a consequence of religious differences.

Case Study 1: India
The Kashmir Dispute in the Indian Sub-Continent

India and Pakistan are two countries united by history and divided by destiny. Their rivalries over five decades have prevented both countries from realising their full economic and political potential. The two countries have fought three wars, two of them over the disputed region of Kashmir. This region is small, but because it is located in the foothills of the Himalayas, its strategic importance and beauty make it a prized possession. Most of Kashmir's population live in a fertile region called 'The Vale of Kashmir' which is intensively cultivated. This vale is surrounded

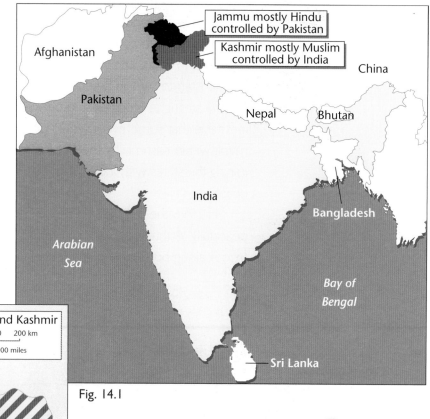

Fig. 14.1

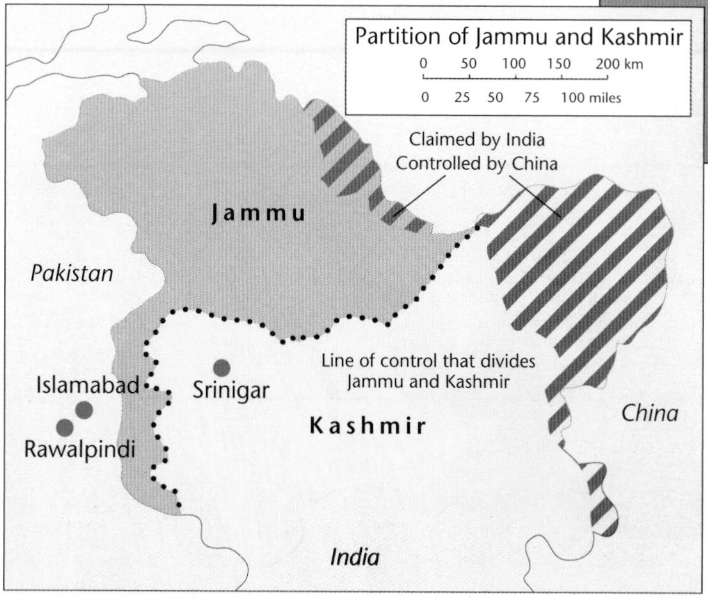

Fig. 14.2

The Punjab state in India is a rich farming region where the Sikh faith dominates, see page 66.

by the high mountains of the Himalayas where few people live and where little agriculture is practised.

The friction between India and Pakistan is relevant to the rest of the world, not only because both countries have nuclear military force, but because it also affects the stability and economic potential of the Indian sub-continent region that includes more than a billion people. The countries' historic dispute over Kashmir will not be resolved easily. The seeds for division were sown when British India was partitioned in 1947.

The Kashmir Dispute

The region called Kashmir is really two states:

- Jammu, which is controlled by Muslim Pakistan and has a Hindu majority population
- Kashmir, which is controlled by Hindu India and has a Muslim majority population.

These two states are divided by a cease-fire line called 'The Line of Control' drawn up by the United Nations in 1949 two years after the war.

In 1947 the sub-continent was divided into two nations based on religious grounds: Pakistan a Muslim state, and India a Hindu state. The leaders of each state within the sub-continent decided whether the state would join with Pakistan or India. However, the division of the sub-continent did not include Jammu and Kashmir because the Maharaja, who was a Hindu, and who ruled both states, had signed agreements with both India and Pakistan to remain neutral.

As strong tensions existed between the two dominant religious groups it was inevitable that some event would occur to upset this neutral position of the Maharaja. A revolt within Kashmir by the Muslim majority against Hindu rule led to the Maharaja joining the states with India. This led to war and a dispute that today has remained unsolved.

In 1996 the Indian and Pakistani prime ministers agreed to settle their dispute peacefully. A threat of war occurred again in 2002 when Pakistan and India amassed troops along both sides of the line of control. Today the conflict continues as before.

> The Indian sub-continent was a colony of Britain up to its partition in 1947.

Kashmir is a mountainous region in the Himalayan range. The Vale of Kashmir is a rich agricultural region within the mountains that has a cooler and more temperate climate than the scorched land of much of India. In this picture women are cropping rice in Kashmir.

This political situation is particularly sensitive for a number of reasons. These include:

- Pakistan and the majority of Muslim people in Kashmir will not accept the line of control as an official border line. The Kashmir region and its large Muslim population hold a very strong emotional pull for the people of Pakistan. They are determined to make Kashmir part of Islamic Pakistan.

- Because much of Pakistan is desert, Pakistan is concerned that the River Indus has several of its main head-streams rising in Indian-controlled Kashmir. The waters of the River Indus and its tributaries are Pakistan's lifelines, because they provide large volumes of clean water for irrigation, and for industrial and domestic uses. Not having control of these head-streams puts Pakistan in a sensitive position.

Access to fresh water supplies is a major concern in India, especially in areas of political conflict.

Case Study 2: Religious Conflict in Northern Ireland

For more than thirty years the words 'Northern Ireland' have created images of violence and bitter sectarian division as Catholics and Protestants have fought each other. Between 1966 and 2000 over 3,600 people have been killed and 36,000 injured as the conflict spread beyond Northern Ireland's borders into Britain and the Irish Republic. Despite this history of violence and mistrust, remarkable steps have recently been taken towards achieving peace. Since 1997, a fragile cease-fire has held among the main paramilitary groups, such as the IRA, the UDA and the UFF. The Good Friday Agreement of 10 April 1998 offers the best hope of a lasting settlement to the violence for well over a generation. The former US Senator George Mitchell was chairman of the all-party peace talks that led to this agreement.

The Roots of the Conflict

The period known as 'The Troubles' is merely one link in a long chain of religious bitterness and conflict stretching back across centuries of Irish history. Since the reign of Henry VIII (1509–49), when Catholic Ireland was brought under Protestant England, tension has existed between the two faiths. During the reign of James I (1603–25) large numbers of Protestants were settled in Northern Ireland as part of the Ulster Plantation, creating a Protestant majority in the region that exists to this day. Following the defeat of the Catholic James II by the Protestant William of Orange at the Battle of the Boyne in 1690, most of the land in Ireland was handed over to Protestant control. The 'Treaty of 1921' after the War of Independence recognised this religious division by dividing the country into two separate political units, a predominantly Catholic south, the Republic of Ireland, and a predominantly Protestant north, Northern Ireland. Most of Northern Ireland's minority Catholic population, do not trust the Protestant majority and would prefer to belong to a single united Ireland. Most of its Protestants, on the other hand, are determined to remain part of the United Kingdom. The result has been an ongoing cycle of protest and violence as paramilitary groups from both sides have sought to press home their point with bombs and guns.

Class activity
1. Name the two states that form the region referred to as 'Kashmir'.
2. Where are these states located?
3. Name the two religious groups that are involved in this dispute.
4. Explain the origins of the dispute.
5. Give two reasons why the region of Kashmir is so important to Pakistan. In your answer, refer to:
   - religion
   - water supplies.

Civil unrest in Northern Ireland generally reaches a peak during the marching season.

The Good Friday Agreement has transformed the politics of Northern Ireland. It created a 108-member assembly and a fourteen-member executive body in which both Catholic and Protestant political representatives sit together in government, only the second time such power sharing has occurred since 1920. The main paramilitary groups are maintaining an uneasy cease-fire, the British military presence is being scaled down, the IRA has begun decommissioning its weapons and foreign money has started to pour into the region as international companies are encouraged by the continuing peace within the North.

Activities

1. When did religious division first take root in Ireland?
2. Which events in the twentieth century created distrust between religious groups in Northern Ireland?
3. What efforts are being made to strengthen trust between both communities today?

Dialogue between the various political groups has led to a cease-fire and peace within Northern Ireland.

Trying to find a compromise between the police and opposing religious groups is often difficult.

However, while some paramilitary groups have for the moment laid aside their weapons, splinter factions such as the republican Real IRA and the loyalist Red Hand Commandos have failed to call a cease-fire. Sectarian violence continues to exist in certain pockets within urban areas and only a small percentage, 52 per cent of Protestants, fully backed the Good Friday Agreement compared to 96 per cent of Catholics. The violence and disorder that regularly erupt between the two communities during the Protestant marching season, and especially during the Twelfth of July anniversary of the 'Battle of the Boyne' is a sign of how far the process has to go before the 'Troubles' are truly a thing of the past.

Class activity

1. Explain the origins of the religious conflict that continues in Ulster today.
2. What political differences today have resulted from this dispute?

TEST YOURSELF AT

my-etest.com

CHAPTER 15
EVERYDAY EXPRESSIONS OF CULTURE AND IDENTITY

Nations and cultural groups express their unique identity through social activities such as sports, traditions, dress code, food, music, art and festivals. Some cultural groups, such as Sikhs, have written codes that they strictly follow, while other groups do so without such individual demands.

GAA sports are an expression of Irish culture and identity.

FESTIVALS AND SPORTS IN IRELAND

More than any other activity, Irish sports, music and art express our unique identity.

Sport

The Gaelic Athletic Association (GAA) has promoted Gaelic hurling and football as their most important sports. Almost every parish throughout the island of Ireland has its own GAA club based on an open membership policy. Everyone is entitled to join and there are no restrictions based on ethnic or religious grounds. The most important events in the GAA are the All-Ireland Finals in Croke Park in Dublin in September each year. GAA sports are played in many countries where Irish emigrants and their descendants live. Such places include the USA, Britain and Australia. Foreign trips to these countries for matches are a regular occurrence for the winners of All-Ireland football and hurling competitions.

However, new traditions also evolve over time. Successful Irish soccer and rugby teams in recent decades have added another dimension to Irish sport. Because these sports are played internationally it allows Irish sports' people to express their national feelings on an international stage. The outward expression of enjoyment of the game and respect for opposing teams has endeared many to our unique identity.

Irish soccer and rugly have offered new opportunities to express our feelings of Irishness.

Music and Dance

Traditional Irish music and dance is a popular expression of Irish culture. 'Lord of the Dance' and Riverdance companies have enhanced this image on a worldwide stage. Feis Ceoil competitions are held each year and these festivals encourage this custom. Special costumes are worn for the participants in these festivals. The designs on female costumes are based on ancient Celtic patterns. Such music and dance competitions are held in cities throughout the world where Irish emigrants and their descendants live today.

Traditional Irish music and dance has led to the creation of many festivals throughout Ireland.

St Patrick's Day parades are held in many cities throughout Ireland and in America.

The Twelfth of July festival expresses a unionist identity in Ireland.

The Wexford Festival caters for those interested in art and opera.

Festivals

There are numerous festivals held in Ireland throughout the year. But the most important ones are held on St Patrick's Day. These festivals give the opportunity to various Irish groups, emigrant groups and cultural groups within Ireland to express themselves and their identity on St Patrick's Day in parades in Irish towns and cities. The most famous **St Patrick's Day Parade** is held on Fifth Avenue in New York and represents the influence of a large Irish-American emigrant population.

The **Twelfth of July** festival expresses the culture and identity of the unionist community in Northern Ireland. It has a British identity. This festival however is regularly associated with outbreaks of violence between the nationalist and the unionist communities in the North and represents the serious divisions that exist between these different cultural groups.

The **Wexford Arts Festival** has grown from small beginnings to one of international standing today. It is based around exhibitions by Irish artists and opera performances for a few weeks during the autumn season. Eisce, another well recognised arts festival is held in Kilkenny.

Many festivals are held throughout Ireland in villages, towns and cities. These may be seasonal festivals in rural communities or based on local amenities, such as angling in Ballina, Co. Mayo.

Find out a bit more about some of these festivals, music or sports.

What music or other cultural festivals are held in your area? Explain.

Class activity
1. Explain how sports, such as gaelic athletics, express our 'Irishness' (a) at home and (b) abroad.
2. Explain how Irish music and dance express 'Irishness' as part of a larger cultural group.

Summer Schools

Many summer schools are held throughout Ireland. These generally attract students from around the world. Their purpose is to promote learning and interaction between students, poets, writers, politicians and university lecturers in an informal setting. Some of these schools include The Merriman School in Ennis, The Humbert School in Mayo and Yeats School in Sligo.

Many foreign and Irish students attend summer schools.

Check the web for information on any of these schools or other summer schools in Ireland.

FESTIVALS AND SPORTS IN EUROPE

Basque Festival

In Pamplona, a city in the Basque region of Spain, an event is held that has made the city famous. Every year, six bulls are allowed to run freely though the city's streets before being killed later that day by matadors in bullfights. Many people run ahead of the bulls some of whom get hurt occasionally.

Munich Beer and Music Festival

The Munich Oktoberfest, known locally as *Wiesen* is the largest public festival in the world. It was first held in 1833 and attracts an average of 6 million visitors each year from all over the world. Over 5 million litres of beer are consumed and one billion Euros are spent during the sixteen days of festivity.

Some people risk their life during the bull running in Pamplona.

Sport

The Finnish people like outdoor sports. In winter they enjoy ice-hockey, ice-skating, ski-jumping and cross-country skiing. Popular summer sports include pesapallo (a Finnish form of baseball), swimming, boating and hiking. In summer, thousands of city families flock to their cottages and saunas on lakes, the coast or the offshore islands.

Name some well-known Irish professional cyclists who have been successful in the Tour de France.

The Munich Beer festival in southern Germany began in 1833.

Cycling

The greatest national sporting event in France is the Tour de France, a bicycle race. Every summer professional cyclists race around almost the entire country. It is broken up into stages and time trials; the race finishes in Paris. Thousands of spectators line the route and cheer them along. Many Irish professional cyclists take part in this race.

In France, boules, a form of bowling, is popular and soccer is the most important team sport.

Boules is a relaxing sport that is played by young and old people in France.

The Tour de France is the greatest cycle race of all. Cyclists reach speeds in excess of 96 km per hour descending from high mountain passes.

Class activity

1. Research one way in which the people of southern Italy and Sicily express their unique identity and culture.
2. Explain why religious and traditional customs in southern Italy have strong ties with the majority of the people of this region.

TEST YOURSELF AT
my-etest.com

SECTION 2
NATIONALITY

KEY IDEA! Nationality and the nation state are political regions placed on the physical and cultural landscape.

Section 2 covers Chapters 16–20. Political geography is the field of study where politics and geography overlap and influence each other. It includes the study of states, their frontiers and boundaries.

It deals also with cultural groups that live within countries. Some of these groups identify with the governments of those areas, while other groups, who are a minority group within a state, feel as if they 'don't belong' and yearn for a nation state of their own. At times some of these groups live in harmony with the majority of the population. On other occasions they may be in conflict with them or their institutions over cultural or political issues.

Many groups who live in the Himalayan Mountains form minority groups within larger nation-states.

The Kurds are an ethnic group. The Iraqi-Kurds seek local self-government within a federal state of Iraq.

The Arab-Israeli conflict has caused many deaths since 1947.

CHAPTER 16
THE NATION-STATE

Fig. 16.1 Identify the countries on the map that became nation-states after the break-up of the former Soviet Union.

The world's nation-states today are represented by lines on a political map of the world, which have evolved over the past 500 years or so. Sixteenth-century Europe, for example, consisted of approximately 1,500 politically independent units. Yet by the beginning of the twenty-first century there were just forty-four nation-states.

The term nation-state implies not only that a country occupies a specific area of land but that this area is occupied by a national group who share a common culture. For example, in France the nation (the people who share a French culture) and the territory of France are virtually the same. This condition applies generally to most of the countries of Europe today. The notable exception here is Belgium which is composed of two distinct national groups: Flemings and Walloons. The former Soviet Union was made-up of many national groups who today form their own nation-states, such as the Ukraine and Belarus.

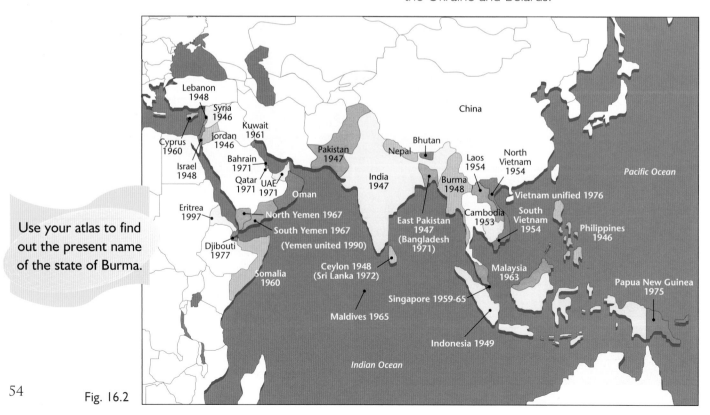

Use your atlas to find out the present name of the state of Burma.

Fig. 16.2

What do we mean by the term nation-state?

It is useful to think of a nation-state as a combination of three elements:

- Nation (ethnicity)
- State (the institution or regime of power)
- Territory (the area enclosed and defined by a political boundary on a map).

A NATION OR NATIONALITY

The idea of nationality emerged shortly after the American and French Revolutions and since then nationalism has become a powerful force in world politics. A nation is a group of people who believe that they are an ethnic community with deep historical roots and the right to own their own sovereign state.

Nationalism is the cause through which such groups claim their right to be a sovereign power within a particular area of land or territory. The invention of the printing press and the creation and standardising of some language dialects, such as Italian, played a leading role in forming national identities.

Although ethnic identity was an important factor in the formation of many nation-states, nations rarely consisted of a single ethnic group. Indeed such states are very rare, Iceland being one of very few such states. Most countries, or nation-states, include more than three ethnic groups within their nations. A major role within mass education has been to integrate diverse ethnic groups and regional minorities into a single community.

Humans are by nature gregarious creatures and group life, no matter how simple or primitive, has some form of social organisation. Into this category of social groups fall the family, the clan, the tribe and the nation.

Some individual sports may represent cultural groups.

Activities
1. Do you think that the images of Ireland are representative of Irish people as a nation today? Explain.
2. What other images of Ireland could you suggest that would give a more balanced representation of Irish people as a nation?

The nation as a group is not easy to define. In fact nationality is vague and yet is incredibly personal and real. It is intangible.

So, the nation can be defined as a group of people who feel bound together through personal ties and who possess a unity and solidarity that has grown up through the following influences:

- By following a common way of life
- By sharing common experiences

- By possessing common cultural traits
- By inheriting a common tradition.

The idea of nationalism – the expression of the sentiments of a group – is not new. What is new is its relationship to the state.

The Criteria for Nationality

Many reasons may be suggested for the creation and maintenance of national feeling, these include race, language, religion and a common enemy.

Race

Belonging to a particular race may produce national feeling, but as we have already discussed there is no such thing as a pure race. Due to widespread migrations over countless centuries the peoples of the world have intermingled so that genetically we are incredibly similar. When race is used as criteria it is usually in the context of superiority. The Nazis, for example, spoke of the superiority of the 'German Race' when, in fact, no German race or even ethnic group existed. The Germans are mostly a mixture of Alpine and Nordic peoples, sub-groups of the Caucasian family. See family groups, page 5.

Language

Language is an important element unifying national groups. It acts as a bonding agent that cements common feelings and traditions that go to make up a grouping such as a nation. It contributes to cultural unity by facilitating the expression of common experience and achievement. It helps people understand each other and removes barriers to taboos that interfere with the communication process.

Religion

Historically religion was important as a moulding influence in politics. The Protestant challenge to the Roman Catholic Church in the sixteenth century helped nationalism since it involved a rejection of foreign influences. In the Protestant countries the churches became largely nationalised, for example, the Anglican Church in England became the official church of the state. In the Republic of Ireland, during most of the twentieth century, the Roman Catholic Church had a close association with the state and its institutions.

Today, religion plays a less significant role in politics, although it is still important in such places as India and Pakistan where religious conflict between Hindus and Muslims continues. This is also true of Israel where Palestinian Muslims and Jewish Israelis are in conflict.

Define the term nation.

Class activity
Explain how the following factors fostered the concept of an Irish nation:
- language
- history
- religion.

Which cultural group or nation does this photograph represent? Explain.

Common enemy

Rivalry, dislike and hatred between two groups will stimulate national feeling. The security of the group will weld its people together and create a united national feeling. This is easily demonstrated by the dislike between the French and the Germans, the Dutch and the Germans, the Finns and the Russians, the Muslims and Hindus, and the Arabs and Jews.

Hindus and Muslims have clashed regularly in the past over religious and political issues.

Activities

1. What is meant by the term nation-state?
2. Explain three factors that help to foster the feeling of nationality.

STATES, THEIR BOUNDARIES AND FRONTIERS

At a glance, the political map of the world shows that it is divided into political units called states or countries, each of which is defined by (enclosed by) a **boundary**. Some of these states are very large while others are tiny.

States are political regions ruled by regimes of power, such as democracies, monarchs or military regimes. Sometimes their **boundaries** conform to physical natural barriers such as rivers, mountain ridges and oceans. However, sometimes they do not and while on a map they may be specific lines, in reality their boundaries are sometimes just undefined and imaginary lines across deserts, plains, farms, lakes and seas.

A **frontier**, on the other hand is a zone or belt of territory, a no-man's-land, which separates one group of people from another. It is sometimes referred to as a border, such as the border between Northern Ireland and the Irish Republic, or the Scottish border, between Scotland and England.

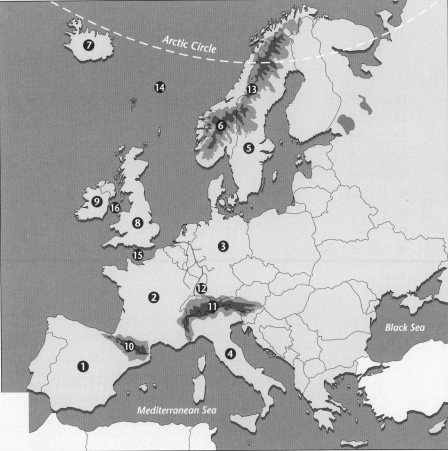

Fig. 16.3

Activity

Carefully examine the map of Europe. Then do the following:
Identify the countries 1–9 and the physical barriers 10–16 that form political boundaries in whole, or in part, between these neighbouring nation-states.

The Principality of Monaco is a tiny state on the Mediterranean coast. Its capital is Monte Carlo.

National Territory

For any state to exist it is essential that it has a certain area of land and a certain minimum of population. A state exists when a feeling is born of collective security. This happens only when groups of people occupying a certain region and using its resources to meet their needs, feel that they have a common bond or inheritance to defend. The presence of other groups of people occupying adjoining territories, who are likely to be rivals or enemies, have been, historically, an important factor in helping to cement such groups to form a nation.

Activity

Carefully examine a map of southern Asia. Then identify the natural physical boundaries that separate:

- India from China
- India from Sri Lanka
- Pakistan from Afghanistan

Be as specific as you can in your answer.

GEOGRAPHICAL SETTING

The Shape, Size and Location of a Nation-State

Where is it, how large is it and what is its shape are three basic questions often asked about a country. Each of these factors are important, especially when other factors such as neighbouring states, boundaries and physical structure are taken into account.

Class activity

Explain the factors that help to define Italy as a nation-state. In your answer refer to

- language
- history
- religion
- physical boundaries.

Shape

The shape of a country can be an advantage or a disadvantage. For example, the more compact the country the better. A circular shape is best, as a circle encloses a large area with a minimum of boundary. No state is circular, but France, for instance, is somewhat circular. At its heart is Paris, with a radial pattern of routes spreading outwards to all parts of the country. Spain is somewhat similar with Madrid at its centre. Others, however, are long and narrow, such as Italy. This has the disadvantage of a core north and a peripheral south. There is some social division between the rich northerners and the poorer southerners from the Mezzogiorno.

In some cases, states are divided into separate units. Pakistan, when it was first created, was divided into East Pakistan on the eastern borders of India and West Pakistan on the western borders of India. Later a civil war created the state of Bangladesh replacing the old state of East Pakistan. Greece and Indonesia are nations made up of many islands. A long shape may create climatic differences leading to isolated peripheral regions such as the cold Norrland region in Sweden.

Read the section on *Shape, Size and Location*.
Then carefully study the map of Germany and
answer the following:
Germany's location, shape and size have offered it
many advantages. Discuss. Use the following
headings to explain your answer:

- Slope of the land
- Physical boundaries
- Natural resources
- Access

Use your atlas to help you with this activity.

Size

Size is important for two reasons.

- Size may create a better sense of national
  security. Russia, for example, was able
  during a number of wars to retreat and
  manoeuvre during invasion to defeat its
  enemy. This happened during the
  Napoleonic Wars and again during World
  War II. Small countries are vulnerable to
  attack, such as Kuwait, which was easily
  overrun by Iraqi forces during the reign of
  Saddam Hussein.

- Large regions usually contain a larger
  supply of natural resources than small
  regions do. Russia, because of its large size
  has almost every possible natural resource.
  This has made it a powerful state. America
  also, has a large area with many climates
  and resources at its disposal.

Fig. 16.4

Germany's River Rhine
is often called the
'Lifeline of Europe'.
Explain this statement.

59

Location

Location involves two factors: absolute location and relative location.

- Absolute location refers to its position on the globe, which is defined by lines of latitude and longitude. This cannot change.

- Relative location may change over time depending on certain factors. In the past, places were isolated because they were inaccessible. This may have been because they were remote islands far from mainland areas, such as Australia, or because they were in a mountainous region. Today, due to the development of air transport, high-speed rail systems and modern ferries, they may no longer be isolated.

Fig. 16.5 Explain, with the aid of this map and your atlas, how the relative location of India has changed over the past century.

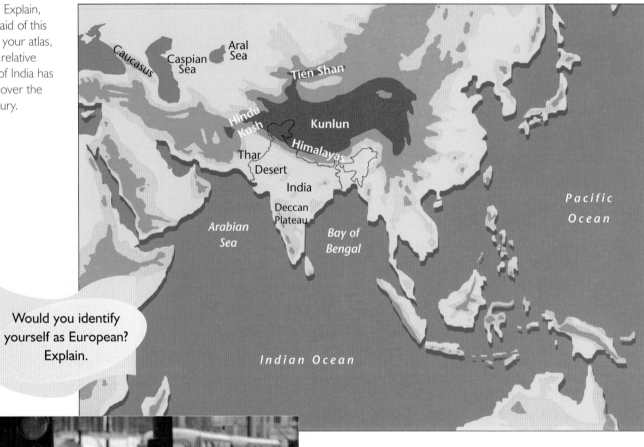

> Would you identify yourself as European? Explain.

European identity includes many diverse ethnic groups.

What makes Europeans, European?

The bonds that Europeans share are supposed to be religion and race, i.e. Christianity and Caucasian. In addition, languages, although different from country to country, evolved from a common Indo-European language. But we know that many Europeans are not Christian. Many Muslims live in France, and Muslims and Hindus live in Britain, because they emigrated from colonies that were or are controlled by France and Britain. As subjects of colonial powers they had the right to citizenship of those countries. So, today, these countries have multicultural societies.

A New Concept of Nationalism

Widespread migration of people from Africa and Asian nations to countries that were not colonial powers is a new phenomenon. The speed at which this is happening is a culture shock and the host nations feel threatened by 'different others'. This new and changing sense of nationalism is one of resistance to new forces of change. Instead of trying to include immigrants, recent trends across the European Union suggest that methods of excluding those that are 'different' are preferred and that a new division of self and other is gaining ground. So the tie between nationality and citizenship may be entering a crisis.

In Europe, where the nation-state first began, the European Union, a supra-national regional state, continues to change the European landscape. Most of Western Europe has been combined within the European Union, while a number of other European states have applied for admission and await entry. Some political analysts see the European Union as the beginning of the end of the territorial nation-state as we have known it. It has undoubtedly led to debate on long-held ideas on what makes a nation.

However, one could look at this another way. There is a new challenge ahead for Europeans. This is to accept that the old sense of nationalism, as expressed in the idea of modern citizenship of the nation-state and as a form of identification, is in decline and is being replaced by the process of European integration. 'So the real danger for the success of an integrated multicultural Europe is the old entrenched cultural nationalism of the nation-state. In other words, and without reducing the threat that mass immigration to Europe may bring, a far more serious problem may be the creation of a "fortress Europe" built on a core set of values belonging to nation-states.'

Underlying every nation-state is the principle of supporting those citizens that are poor and on the fringe of society. Western democracies support this principle. However, recent immigration trends to Europe have created fears that Western democracies may be unable to cope with the demand on welfare, as many immigrants are viewed as liabilities, rather than as intelligent people with the same hopes and desires that European emigrants had when they emigrated to the New World.

Some people fear that mass migration may create a strain on national government as well as social conflict.

Many in Ireland view new migrants as refugees who deserve a new life with all the rights as laid down by the UN charter.

Class activity

1. Explain the meaning of nationalism.
2. Explain how a sense of nationalism can lead to a fear of 'different others'.
3. Explain how the location, shape and size of Ireland has helped create: (a) a nation-state and (b) a sense of nationalism.

TEST YOURSELF AT

CHAPTER 17
ISSUES RELATING TO PHYSICAL AND POLITICAL BOUNDARIES

This chapter deals with issues that relate to each of the following topics:
- Physical and political boundaries
- Cultural groups within nation-states
- Cultural groups without nationality
- Conflicts between political structures and cultural groups.

Physical boundaries follow natural features in the physical environment, such as rivers, mountain ridges, lakes and seas. Rivers are easily recognised as boundaries, but river channels may change location due to meandering. The United States and Mexico have negotiated the boundary along the Rio Grande, called Rio Bravo in Mexico, numerous times in the twentieth century to reflect changes in the location of the river's channel.

Activity
Examine a physical map of Britain and Ireland in your atlas. Then identify the physical boundaries that separate
- Scotland from England
- Wales from England
- Ireland from Scotland
- Ireland from England and Wales.

Low river water levels in Pakistan regularly lead to disputes with its neighbour India over irrigation-scheme projects.

WATER SUPPLIES

One of the issues most likely to lead to conflict between neighbouring countries will concern the management of fresh water supplies. The importance of international rules that govern the allocation of these waters cannot be overemphasised. Worldwide there are more than 300 major river basins, covering about 50 per cent of the world's total land area. Many of these basins straddle country borders, even more so today due to the break up of the former Soviet Union and Eastern Europe. Examples of river basins straddling more than one state include the Nile River, with nine countries sharing the basin, and the Danube River in Europe, shared by seventeen countries.

The potential for water conflicts over trans-boundary waters is clear, especially in times of water scarcity. Is the upstream state entitled to use all of the water that originates in its territory? Are the existing developments, such as irrigation schemes, of downstream states protected against later use of their upstream neighbours?

Case Study: River Indus (India/Pakistan)

The River Indus begins in Tibet in China, with India and Pakistan being the downstream users. The partition of India and Pakistan by the British disrupted an irrigation system that had been in place for over 5,000 years. This led to conflict between India and Pakistan when India withheld water flows to canals in Pakistan. It was only through the intervention of the World Bank that the countries could reach agreement. Since then the countries have tried to settle their disputes through peaceful means.

> Look at a map of South Asia. Then focus on the River Indus. Find its head-streams, see where they rise and follow their courses until they meet the River Indus. Now explain why the use of these waters is of concern to India and Pakistan.

OFFSHORE BOUNDARIES

Boundaries between states are understood to extend above surface, beneath it, and for those with coastlines, offshore. The water, seabed and their resources, such as oil and gas, within 200 nautical miles of the seashore belongs exclusively to that country. This area is called a country's Exclusive Economic Zone (EEZ). Territorial seas, over which states have virtually the same authority as over land, extend twelve nautical miles offshore. States, however, must allow 'innocent passage' of foreign ships through these waters.

Problems with locating political boundaries are common because many coastal states, such as Denmark, Germany and Sweden, are not separated by 400 nautical miles of ocean. So, lines halfway between the nearest shorelines of adjoining states must be defined. Such formal boundaries must go through a series of stages for agreement before they become legal. Beyond EEZs lie the high seas, open to all states for transport and resource development.

Coastal waters are a major natural resource. Many foreign ships fish illegally in Ireland's EEZ. This trawler is one of two Japanese ships that was apprehended by the Irish Navy off Castletownbere.

Mineral rights on continental shelves provide vast sources of oil and gas for some nations such as Norway and Britain.

Activity
Explain why the passage of some vessels through territorial waters would be of concern to every nation with a coastal location. In your explanation refer to
- Military vessels
- Fishing vessels
- Transport ships.

Activity

Study Fig. 17.1. Then explain the importance of seabed ownership in the North Sea to

● Norway
● Britain
● Netherlands

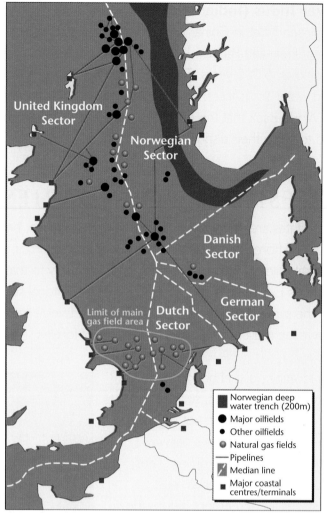

Fig. 17.1

Class activity

Read page 65. Then do the following:

1. Explain what is meant by the term 'border'.

2. Explain why six counties and not four counties formed a political unit called Northern Ireland.

3. Explain why the 'border' was not an effective or suitable boundary, either socially or economically, between the two states.

POLITICAL BOUNDARIES

The boundaries of a state define its ability to enforce its laws. Laws, whether on taxation or criminal activities, can be enforced only within the area defined by its political boundaries. As a result individuals may place their money in a bank in another state where tax laws are less costly, such as in Switzerland, in the Cayman Islands or elsewhere. Agreements between states have made hiding 'hot' money less secure and extradition treaties between countries have made the return of criminals and their assets less troublesome.

Governments use borders (boundaries between countries) to control the flow of goods, people, money and communications both into and out of the state. Relationships with bordering states are managed along international guidelines, but political decisions on how they function may change from government to government.

Effects of Political Boundaries on Cultural Groups

The boundaries of most modern African states are the result of European colonial powers, such as France, Portugal, the United Kingdom and Spain, dividing up Africa at the Berlin Conference in 1884–85, to benefit themselves, without concerns for the homelands of the hundreds of African ethnic groups. A continuing legacy of these 'artificial' boundaries has been ethnic conflict.

In Rwanda and Burundi, for example, the rivalry between Hutus and Tutsis resulted in hundreds of thousands of deaths in 1994. In Nigeria in the late 1960s over 1 million people died as the Ibo ethnic group attempted to create a separate state of their own.

Case Study 2: Partition on the Island of Ireland

The 'border' between Northern Ireland and the Republic of Ireland has its origins in the creation of the Irish Free State in 1921, after the War of Independence. A Boundary Commission was set up to decide where the frontier should be drawn between the British statelet of Northern Ireland and the newly independent Irish Free State, which went on to become the Irish Republic in 1948.

Northern Protestants, called unionists because of their support for wishing to remain part of Britain, had a clear majority over Catholics in only four northern counties – Antrim, Down, Derry and Armagh. This was deemed too small a territory to form a viable unionist state, so the predominantly Catholic counties of Fermanagh and Tyrone were added to the province of Northern Ireland.

Fig. 17.2

- Three of Ulster's counties – Donegal, Cavan and Monaghan – were now in the Irish Free State. The remainder were in British-controlled Northern Ireland.
- Countless farms were divided between the Irish Free State and Northern Ireland.
- The city of Derry, now in Northern Ireland, was cut off from its natural hinterland of Donegal.
- Many people were unhappy with this division. Both Protestant unionists stranded on the Irish Republic side of the border and Catholic nationalists trapped on the Northern Ireland side felt betrayed by this political boundary. The Boundary Commission surveyed residents of the border areas to gauge their wishes, but concluded in 1925 that any changes would not be compatible with economic and physical considerations.
- The division led to the violence of the IRA, the UDA and other paramilitary groups in Northern Ireland.

Revise the section on the dispute over the political boundary of Jammu and Kashmir, page 46.

Explain why military posts such as this were built along the border that separates Northern Ireland from the Irish Republic.

TEST YOURSELF AT
my-etest.com

The border created divisions within the island of Ireland. Give two examples of this division.

CHAPTER 18
CULTURAL GROUPS WITHIN NATION-STATES

Many Turks came to Germany to work as 'Gastarbeiters' or guest workers.

Case Study 1: Turks in Germany

There are 1.8 million Turks in Germany, 139,000 of them in Berlin alone, making them the largest group of foreign workers. In your elective you studied these 'Gastarbeiters' or guest workers. They were recruited to do low-paid jobs in Germany that the educated middle-class Germans would not do from 1961 onwards. The migrants dreamed of earning money and retiring to a small business and a secure life back in Turkey. Many of their families joined them in Germany. In 1973 after the oil crisis, recruitment stopped, and many did go home. But the population of Turks in Germany has been kept high because many remained, family members continued to come from Turkey and the high birth rate among this ethnic group.

Many Turks of the second and third generations born or raised in Germany have little knowledge of Turkey. Turkey has a similar status to what Ireland had for Irish-Americans, kept alive by a myth of final return, particularly among the first generation who came to Germany as adults. They plan for a retirement that will take them back to Turkey for good, but more and more older German Turks are retiring in Germany. They want to be close to their children and grandchildren. The second and third generations show little sign of wanting to 'return' to a place and a culture with which they are increasingly unfamiliar.

There is a high percentage of school-going German youths of Turkish origin. This increases educational costs for the state, as their home language is Turkish, a language derived from Arabic.

Case Study 2: Sikhs

The Sikhs are a cultural group who belong to a religion that was founded by Guru Nanak about 500 years ago to unite Muslims and Hindus of all castes into a single faith. This faith gained millions of followers in the Punjab region. Guru Nanak taught there was one, universal god. Their holiest shrine is the Golden Temple in Amritsar. During colonial rule many Sikhs won the respect and trust of the British and many thousands were employed as policemen and soldiers. As a result a large Sikh middle class developed in the rich agricultural region called the Punjab.

The culture of the Sikhs is largely affected by their religious beliefs and every important Sikh ceremony is performed in the presence of the Holy Granth (Sikh Bible).

In order to unite Hindus and Muslims the Sikh faith asked its followers to throw off all divisions of caste, colour and race. As members of the same cultural group all Sikhs resemble each other by wearing five symbols, called the 'K' symbols. They are:

- 'Kesh' (uncut hair)
- 'Kangha' (wooden comb)
- 'Karra' (steel bracelet)
- 'Kachha' (short breeches)
- 'Kirpaan' (blade 6" to 9") to symbolise self-respect.

Sikh male adults wear a **dastar**, or turban, to show their commitment to Sikhism. Turbans are made from a piece of material five metres long and one metre wide that is turned clockwise around the head six times. Sikh women are also required to cover their heads, usually with a long scarf called a **chunni**. Sikhs who follow all of these conditions are called **Khalsa**. People who follow only some of these requirements are called **Sahajdharis**.

Sikhs are clearly different from other Indians in their appearance and dress code. This symbol of distinct identity is called **bana**. Many Sikhs seek independence from India. In order to satisfy this demand the Indian government made Punjab a separate Punjabi-speaking state where the Sikhs are the majority rulers. However, many Sikhs want full independence in a newly renamed state they call Khalistan.

Class activity

1. Explain the economic and social factors that led to the creation of a Turkish cultural group within Germany.
2. Explain why Sikhs form a cultural group within India. In your answer refer to
   - religion
   - dress
   - language.

Name the characteristics that identify these people as Sikhs.

Identify the traditional dress code of this Sikh woman.

Compare the differences that distinguish the Indian females in this picture from the Sikh women in the other pictures.

TEST YOURSELF AT
my-etest.com

CHAPTER 19
CULTURAL GROUPS WITHOUT NATIONALITY

Many cultural groups do not have a nation-state of their own. They live as a minority group within a nation-state. Examples of such groups include the Basques in Spain and nationalists in Northern Ireland.

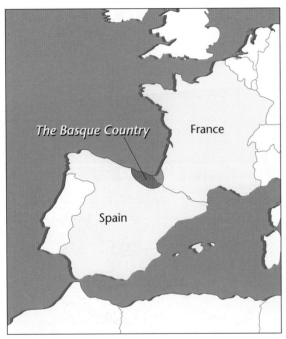

Fig. 19.1 Part of the Basque region lies in Spain. The other part lies in France.

Case Study 1: The Basques

The Basque country is a region that covers an area of 20,644 square kilometres at the western end of the Pyrenees, the mountains that divide France from Spain. It is made up of seven districts, four of which are in Spain and form the largest section, while the other three are in France. Three of these historic Basque territories, Araba, Bizkaia and Gipuzkoa in the north of Spain, are grouped together to form a political unit, known as **Euskadi**, or the Autonomous Community of the Basque Country. **Euskadi** has a population of 2.1 million people with an average population density of 300 people per square kilometre, higher than the EU average. They have their own president and parliament but are represented internationally by Spain.

Spain's other Basque district, Navarra, is its own region, separate from Euskadi and is less troubled politically. The people, about 200,000 of them in the Basque districts in France are culturally distinct but completely a part of France.

The scenic landscape of the Basque region adds to its attraction for tourists.

Class activity

1. Define the 'absolute' location of the Basque region.
2. Identify the territories that form Euskadi.
3. What is meant by 'Autonomous Community of the Basques'?
4. How does the Basque region of Navarra differ from Euskadi?

Who are the Basques and why are they different?

The Basques are a very old cultural group. They were living in the Pyrenees over 4,000 years ago, long before the Celtic tribes of central Europe moved west to Britain and Ireland. They speak Basque, which they call Euskara, a language unrelated to any other human tongue. So it is not Indo-European. It has many different dialects. Basques also speak Spanish or French. Some speak both.

Basques are dark in complexion, though not as dark as most French people or Spaniards of this region.

What do they do?

Traditionally, the Basques were herders. Today, Spain's Basque region has many businesses. Bilbao, the region's largest city is known for its steel plants and shipbuilding yards based on its coal and iron ore supplies. The region has a positive Science and Technology Plan to strengthen this type of business and industry. Most people live in the larger urban areas. France's Basque region is more rural.

What do they eat?

Basque cuisine is based on seafood, especially cod and hake, a type of whitefish, and squid cooked in its own ink sauce. Basque dishes are very popular throughout Spain and most major cities have Basque restaurants.

A tradition

This is an event that has made Pamplona, a city in Navarra, famous. Every year, six bulls are allowed to run freely through the city's streets before being killed later that day by matadors in a bullfight. Many people run ahead of the bulls and sometimes get hurt or killed.

The Pyrenees ... a Political Frontier

The Pyrenees is a physical barrier between Spain and France. However, there are many passes through these mountains and both ends to the north and south allow access for roads and railways. At the northern end the Basque region reaches into both states, while the Catalan region in the south lies on both sides of the mountains. So the mountains do not form a complete barrier, but have nevertheless served as a successful boundary between both countries.

Pamplona is a major tourist town and is associated with the running of the bulls in a summer festival.

Shipbuilding is one of the Basque's most traditional employers. Its local coal and iron ore deposits led to the creation of this industrial activity.

The Basque region in Spain is fast becoming an important tourist destination within Spain.

NATIONALISTS IN NORTHERN IRELAND

People who live in Northern Ireland and wish to be part of a united Ireland are called nationalists. Since partition, nationalists have lived under British rule and until recent times have suffered discrimination on many fronts. They are Irish in their traditions and customs and feel a strong sense of being Irish, rather than being British as unionists do. Most nationalists are Catholics and are represented by political organisations such as the SDLP or Sinn Fein.

Some nationalists show their identity by displaying Irish symbols on their houses.

The nationalist population developed their sense of Irishness, just as the majority of the people of the Irish Republic did, as a consequence of the British occupation of the island of Ireland and the treatment at the hands of the British Forces and Royal Ulster Constabulary (Northern Ireland's police force). The events of 1916–21 and the oppressive treatment of the Catholic minority for over seventy years have cemented nationalist feelings that created an Irish identity.

The demand for civil rights and equal treatment with Protestant citizens led to civil rights marches in the 1960s and 1970s. These marches led to clashes between police and marchers that reached a peak in the shooting dead of thirteen unarmed civilians by the British Forces on what is now called 'Bloody Sunday' in the city of Derry. Over 20,000 people gathered in Derry in 2002 to mark the thirtieth anniversary of this atrocity.

A minority of extreme nationalists support the IRA, an illegal armed organisation. At present a cessation of military activities is part of the peace process that continues to dominate Northern politics today.

The distribution patterns of the urban population of Catholics and Protestants has led to 'ghettos' in cities such as Derry and Belfast. Ethnic clashes between Catholic and Protestant 'ghetto communities' regularly continue to occur.

Nationalists are generally Catholics who often campaign for civil liberties on the streets of towns in Northern Ireland.

Class activity
1. Explain how British rule in Ireland helped create the Irish nation.
2. Explain the factors that led to civil rights marches in Northern Ireland in the 1960s and 1970s.
3. Explain how gerrymandering affected nationalists' civil rights in Northern Ireland. (See page 44.)

TEST YOURSELF AT
my-etest.com

CHAPTER 20
CONFLICTS BETWEEN NATIONAL GOVERNMENTS AND CULTURAL GROUPS

Violence breaks out regularly between cultural groups and the governments of their nation-states. This violence generally occurs because of injustice, lack of civil liberties, religious persecution or a demand for independence. In many cases it's a mixture of some or all of these factors.

THE IRA AND THE BRITISH GOVERNMENT IN NORTHERN IRELAND

Since Ireland was partitioned, a minority group, called the IRA, has waged a guerrilla war to unite the whole island of Ireland into a single state. For many years, and for as many reasons, the activities of the IRA were on a small scale. Conflict between them and the British government was confined to occasional clashes and raids on arms supplies. Then, due to the indifference for equality and civil rights for Catholics in Northern Ireland on the part of the British government, the IRA renewed its campaign in the 1960s. The demand for basic rights – to jobs, housing, voting – threw the six counties into a state of crisis. The peaceful demand for civil rights was met with violence from the British forces and the police. This violence reached its peak during a peace rally in January 1972, later known as Bloody Sunday. Thirteen people were shot dead and many others injured when the British Army fired on the marchers.

The bombing of Omagh by the Real IRA created public outrage from all sections of society in Northern Ireland and the Irish Republic.

Consequently the IRA intensified its campaign and focused its attention on a bombing campaign in British cities and army barracks in Northern Ireland and along the border region. The introduction of internment, prison without trial, intensified the campaign. This led to the deaths of ten IRA volunteers who went on hunger strike, to highlight their claim for political status rather than criminal status within Northern jails.

Sectarian violence between Catholics and Protestants also led to IRA activity. Eventually both the IRA and the British Army admitted that military victory for either side was not possible. Finally the ending of 'military operations' in 1994 by the IRA was a result of the Irish Peace Initiative led by SDLP leader John Hume and Sinn Fein leader, Gerry Adams, and supported by the Irish, British and American governments. Peace talks continue.

The majority of Basques seek more autonomy within their region by peaceful means.

Activity
- Who are Sinn Fein?
- Who do they represent?
- Who do people believe they represent?
- What is internment?
- Write a brief profile of Gerry Adams and Martin McGuinness.

THE SPANISH GOVERNMENT AND THE BASQUES

As mentioned on page 68, the Basques are a cultural group who live at the western end of the Pyrenees in Spain and France.

A small number of violent extremists are represented by ETA. ETA (in Basque it means Basque Homeland and Freedom) is an armed nationalist group who believe that complete independence from Spain and France can only be achieved by military means, similar to what the IRA believed about the reunification of Ireland. Initially ETA was founded in 1958 because the Basque people were oppressed during the reign of the fascist dictator Franco in Spain. Because they were 'different' he saw them as a threat and he tried to eliminate all political opposition to his rule.

In the beginning they were a non-violent group but their every move for independence was put down by force. This made them opt for armed resistance.

The influence of ETA on Basque society is not measured only by the impact of its armed struggle. A key concept of ETA is the 're-nationalisation of the Basque country' – to restore the Basque region to its full cultural personality. This has had a great impact on the social, political and cultural life of the Basque region. However, ETA is not represented in power sharing in government like their role model in Ireland, the IRA. So ETA has returned to the very methods it discarded as hopeless in 1998, after years when terrorist violence proved unsuccessful in achieving greater economic and political independence from Spain's central government.

In addition Basque nationalism has risen in France, an area that was originally stable. Policy changes on social conditions and welfare and the loss of influence by trade unions has led to discontent. Remember, that ETA seeks complete independence from Spain by military means.

ETA seek complete independence from Spain by military means.

Class activity
1. Explain the factors that allowed the IRA to intensify its campaign of violence in Northern Ireland.
2. Who are ETA? Explain why ETA intensified its campaign of violence in Spain.
3. What similarities, if any, exist between the campaigns of violence waged by ETA and the IRA?

TEST YOURSELF AT
my-etest.com

SECTION 3
IDENTITY

 **KEY IDEA!**

Identity involves a variety of cultural factors, such as nationality, language, race and religion.

Section 3 draws together the issues of race, nationality and identity already discussed in the previous chapters. Germany is taken as a case study as it was dealt with in Chapter 28 in *Our Dynamic World 1* as an example of a region whose changing political boundaries had an impact on some of its cultural groups.

Soccer is the most popular team sport in Germany.

Music has a long and proud association with the German people.

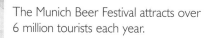

The Munich Beer Festival attracts over 6 million tourists each year.

CHAPTER 21
CASE STUDY: GERMANY

GERMANY'S PHYSICAL AND POLITICAL BOUNDARIES

This region was studied in 'Regional Geography' in *Our Dynamic World 1*.

Germany has a number of well-defined natural boundaries. These are best defined in the north, east, south-east, south and south-west border areas. Only on the western edge is the boundary less well defined. Northern Germany forms part of the North European Plain, which is a natural region in Western Europe. Southern Germany forms part of an upland region that was uplifted due to earth movements at the same time as the Alps were formed. The crushing movement created by the collision of the African and Eurasian Plates was less severe in Germany than it was in Italy and Switzerland and so its uplands are not as high as the Alps that define its southern borders.

Germany's political borders used natural features where possible, such as the River Rhine that separates France from Germany, the River Oder that separates it from Poland, the Bohemian Forest uplands that divide it from the Czech Republic, and the Alps that divide it from Austria and Switzerland. The Baltic and North Seas separate Germany from its northern neighbours, with the exception of Denmark to which it is connected by a narrow stretch of lowland.

Fig. 21.1

Class activity
Explain how the following factors helped create the German nation-state:
- physical boundaries
- language.

OLD AND NEW POLITICAL BOUNDARIES OF GERMANY

Old Boundaries

The present German nation has its beginnings in the German Empire in 1871. It ended with World War I in 1914. Its leader was called 'The Kaiser' and his name was William I of Prussia. Otto von Bismark was prime minister. It was a federal state where each state ruled itself, except in certain matters reserved for government in Berlin. Its area was larger than that of today's Germany. It included Alsace-Lorraine, a region of present-day France and all north-western and western regions of present-day Poland.

Since World War I Germany has played a pivotal role in the shaping and reshaping of Western Europe. It is a country centrally located at the heart of Europe and it is the most powerful economy in the European Union.

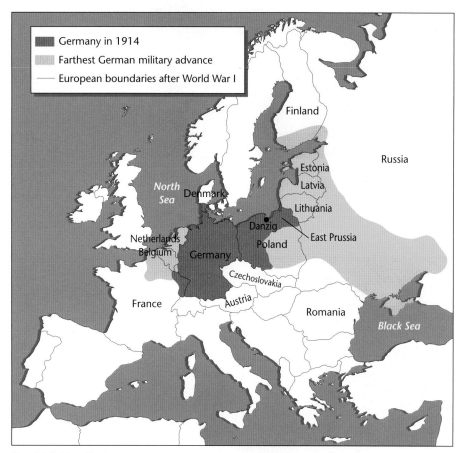

Fig. 21.2 Identify the nation-states on the map that were captured by Germany during World War I.

RELIGIOUS CONFLICT WITHIN THE GERMAN EMPIRE

About one-third of the people of the new German Empire were Catholic, the rest of the people were Protestant. Protestantism was a faith begun by the teachings of **Martin Luther in 1517,** which you studied in your Junior Certificate History. To protect their interests, German Catholics organised themselves into a new party, called the 'Centre Party'. They opposed the creation of the German Empire and demanded a firm guarantee of the freedom of the Catholic Church in the new Germany. At the same time Pope Pius IX proclaimed **papal infallibility** to be a doctrine of faith. This meant that when ruling on matters of faith or morals, he was inspired by God and could not make a mistake. Bismarck felt this 'infallibility' issue would lead to interference by the Church in state matters.

Some of the Catholics believed in this rule while others did not. This division, called 'kulturkampf' among the Catholics, was used by **Bismarck** to crush all opposition to his rule. He introduced **The May Laws** which restricted the influence of the Church in the

Bavarian houses set in upland have verandas and potted plants which are typical of this region.

running of the German state. The powers of the clergy were restricted and priests were not allowed to raise political topics in their sermons. Civil marriages were made compulsory. By 1876 all bishops were either in prison or in exile and over one-third of the 4,600 Catholic parishes were without a priest. Many of these laws were withdrawn after 1879 when a new Pope was elected and new agreements were signed.

POLITICAL BOUNDARY CHANGES AFTER WORLD WAR I

The Versailles Treaty

Prior to World War I, most of Europe was controlled by empires, with kings and queens as their rulers. Many of these royal families were related through marriages and so their countries had close economic and social ties. An attack on one was seen as an attack on the other. Hatreds also existed and this created divisions between some of these empires. When the Archduke Franz Ferdinand of Austria was assassinated in Sarajevo, Germany, under the leadership of Kaiser William II, was brought into World War I in support of Austria. Austria and Germany were opposed in the war by Russia, Britain and France. After the war, the German Empire had fallen and Germany had lost all of its lands in Poland and Alsace-Lorraine in France. New boundary lines were drawn to reflect these changes and the River Rhine now formed the boundary between France

Germany in 1939
Farthest German military advance
European boundaries after WW II

Fig. 21.3 Identify the countries occupied by Germany during World War II.

and Germany. Under the **Treaty of Versailles** no German troops were allowed to enter the 'Rhineland' to ensure a secure border for France in this region.

Changing Boundaries under Hitler

Adolf Hitler was a violent and ambitious man. He wanted to make Germany the most powerful country in Europe. In order to do this he invaded neighbouring countries and took them over by force. Hitler had three main aims.

The influence of language

Hitler wanted to unite all German-speaking people into one single nation-state. There were many German-speaking people in parts of Poland, Czechoslovakia and Austria. Hitler wanted to bring these people under the control of Germany.

Racial policy

Hitler regarded Germans as a master race of people, superior to all others. He wanted to rid a greater Germany of all others who were inferior and could dilute this breed by intermarriage. So marriage between ethnic groups, such as Jews and Germans, was forbidden.

More living space

Hitler wanted to create more living space for Germans. He believed the Treaty of Versailles had robbed Germany of much of her territory. So he wanted Germany to have parts of Czechoslovakia, Austria, Poland and Russia. This would give the German people more farmland for growing foodstuffs and raw materials for vital industries.

As a result of Hitler's policies, Germany invaded Austria in 1938. Later in 1939, the Germans invaded Czechoslovakia and in September 1939, they invaded Poland. The invasion of Poland led to the outbreak of World War II. These invasions increased the area of Germany and changed its political boundaries again. They lasted until the ending of the war in 1945.

Class activity
1. Explain the historical factors that led to the Versailles Treaty.
2. Explain how national feeling in Germany was affected by the Versailles Treaty.
3. What part did Adolf Hitler play in changing national feeling during the 1930s?

See 'Racial Conflict' page 16.

NEW BOUNDARIES

From 1949 to 1990 new political boundaries were drawn in Germany. At the end of World War II Germany was divided by the Allied Powers. Three zones occupied by Western powers were united to form the country of West Germany, which was called the Federal Republic of Germany. The USSR created the new state of East Germany from the zone that it controlled, which was called the German Democratic Republic.

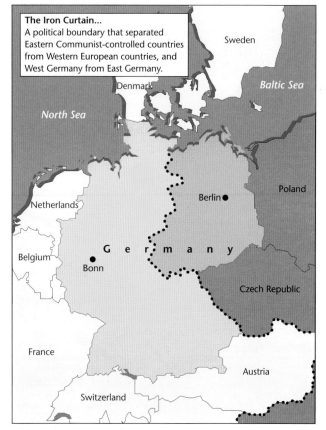

The Iron Curtain...
A political boundary that separated Eastern Communist-controlled countries from Western European countries, and West Germany from East Germany.

Fig. 21.4

Millions of Jews were killed during the Holocaust. Concentration camps were set up to separate Jews from society at large.

The removal of the Berlin Wall was followed by the reunification of Germany.

Berlin, the historic capital of Germany, was also divided. East Berlin became the capital of East Germany. West Berlin was an outpost of West Germany deep within the East German state. In 1961, the East Germans built the Berlin Wall to divide the city and set up military checkpoints to control the movements of people from East to West Berlin. This wall symbolised the division between East and West during the Cold War, which you studied in your Junior Certificate History course.

In 1990 East and West Germany were reunited, the Berlin Wall was removed and the German people felt they were a nation once more.

Consequences of Changing Political Boundaries
Changing citizenship

Germany's current eastern boundary corresponds roughly to the one of the Holy Roman Empire in the tenth century, because many areas of Europe that were formerly German speaking, now lie behind political boundaries outside of Germany. For example, Alsace-Lorraine is now a part of France; the northern reaches of Schleswig-Holstein are in Denmark; parts of East Prussia are in Lithuania and Russia; West Prussia, Posen, Silesia, and the Pomerania are in Poland.

However, political boundaries change. Elsass was called Alsace when it became French in the seventeenth century. It became German again in 1871, French again in 1919, German again in 1940, and French again in 1945. Therefore, an American whose ancestors arrived in 1869 might be classified Franco-American, even though his ancestors spoke predominantly German.

In earlier centuries, Austria and South Tyrol, Switzerland, Liechtenstein and Luxembourg, parts of Russia and the Balkan countries were within the boundaries of Germany. So people from these regions could up until recent times claim German citizenship immediately, once within Germany's political boundaries. These people are referred to as **ethnic Germans** or German-Americans. It is unclear when or why this term is used for such immigrants.

Wars

Germany went to war on two separate occasions in the twentieth century. These wars, World War I and World War II, cost millions of lives. On each occasion Germany invaded its neighbours in order to increase its territory. However, it lost both wars. Germany was divided into two separate states, The **German Democratic Republic** (East Germany) and the **Federal Republic of Germany** (West Germany) as a consequence of World War II. It was not to be reunited again until 1990.

Many German cities and industrial areas suffered great damage during World War II.

ETHNICITY AND RACE

Hitler believed that German people were of a superior race to all other humans. He wrote that they would stay 'pure' by avoiding marriage to Jews and Slavs. However, as you have studied in your elective, there is no such thing as a pure race. Europeans, including Germans, belong to the Caucasian ethnic group as you studied in Chapter 1 of this book. Caucasian refers to Europeans and people of European ancestry and brown-skinned peoples, such as Arabs and people of the Indian sub-continent. Hitler's view of 'others' as different led to racial persecution and the death of over 6 million Jews during the Holocaust.

Ethnic Groups within Germany – the Role of Migration
Who are ethnic Germans?

Ethnic Germans are descendants of Germans who lived in lands in Eastern Europe and Russia that had at one time been German territory. These ethnic Germans had the right to German citizenship according to Germany's constitution. Because they became citizens immediately upon arrival in Germany, ethnic Germans received financial and social assistance to ease their integration into German society. Because they came from many different countries they did not speak German and so even language training was provided. Generally they were readily accepted into German society.

However, with the fall of Communism and the removal of the Iron Curtain the number of ethnic Germans swelled. In the mid-1980s about 40,000 came each year. In the period 1991–93, about 400,000 ethnic Germans settled in Germany. Since January 1993, immigration of ethnic Germans has been limited to 220,000 per year.

Because this mass immigration could no longer be managed, especially because of the vast expense of unification, restrictions on the right of ethnic Germans to return to Germany became effective in 1991. Under the new restrictions, once in Germany ethnic Germans must live in certain areas. If they leave these areas, they lose many of their benefits and are treated as if they are foreigners. Although ethnic Germans are entitled to German citizenship, to many Germans they do not seem German, and their social integration has frequently been difficult.

Although officially German, ethnic Germans are poor, have little or no knowledge of the German language, and prefer to remain in their own social group. They form a cultural group within Germany.

Much rebuilding and renewal has taken place in Berlin since reunification. However, reunification has created some difficulties for the German people. Identify two such problems.

Class activity
1. Explain why Hitler's belief in a superior race has no foundation scientifically or otherwise.
2. Who are ethnic Germans?
3. Explain how ethnic Germans became a financial burden on the German state in recent decades.

Some Germans fear that eastern Germans may become a major strain on Germany's finances and so create a lower living standard throughout the western part of Germany.

Ossies and Wessies

After reunification in Germany in 1990, many industries in the former East Germany were exposed to competition from more efficient industries of the West. Many were forced to close creating mass unemployment. Because they were now living in a democracy, East Germans had the choice of migrating to West Germany, where there are better employment prospects. Within three years of reunification, over 3 million people had migrated to West Germany. But they were not that welcome when they arrived. Many felt they were treated as second-class citizens in their own country. This discrimination led to the terms *Ossies*, meaning East Germans and *Wessies*, referring to West Germans.

Ossies resented the superior attitude of the wealthier West Germans and also felt that the Wessies had not done enough to secure them employment in their own eastern region.

Wessies, on the other hand, resented the fact that their taxes were increased to support the unemployed Ossies. Increased migration from eastern Germany put pressure on housing and employment supplies in western Germany. A belief that Ossies were lazy and ungrateful was also common among the wealthier Wessies.

Turks in Germany

Class activity

1. Explain how the reunification of Germany has led to social division in Germany.
2. Explain why some foreign nationals in Ireland should be granted citizenship based on social justice.

There are 1.8 million Turks in Germany, 139,000 of them in Berlin alone, making them the largest group of foreign workers. In your elective you studied about these 'Gastarbeiters' or guest workers. They were recruited to do low-paid jobs in Germany that the educated middle-class Germans would not do from 1961 onwards. The migrants dreamed of earning money and retiring to a small business and a secure life back in Turkey. Many of their families joined them in Germany. In 1973 after the oil crisis, recruitment stopped, and many did go home. But because many remained, and many family members continued to come from Turkey, and there is a high birth rate among this ethnic group, the population of Turks in Germany has remained high.

Many Turks of the second and third generations born or raised in Germany have little knowledge of Turkey. Turkey has the status similar to what Ireland has for Irish-Americans, kept alive by a myth of final return, particularly among the first generation who came to Germany as adults. They plan for retirement that will take them back to Turkey for good. But more and more older German Turks are retiring in Germany. They want to be close to their children and grandchildren, the second and third generations, who show little sign of returning to a place and a culture with which they are increasingly unfamiliar.

Case Study: Ethnic Conflict

Skinheads convicted of German race murder
30 August 2000

Halle, Germany – Three racists have been convicted of murder for the fatal beating of a Mozambican man – a crime that focused national attention on a rising wave of violence against foreign nationals in Germany.

The state court in Halle sentenced Enrico Hilprecht, 24, to the maximum of life in prison for the brutal attack.

His two 16-year-old co-defendants, Christian Richter and Frank Miethbauer, were each given sentences of nine years, one year less than the maximum allowed for juveniles.

Prosecutors had sought the maximum sentences for all three, charging they had acted out of hatred for foreign nationals when they went after Alberto Adriano on 11 June, kicking and beating him so brutally that he died from his injuries three days later.

Reading the verdict, Judge Albrecht Hennig said the court came to the conclusion that the three killed Adriano solely because of the colour of his skin.

'It was the latest in the long chain of attacks to which we must put an end', Hennig said.

The defendants looked stone-faced as the verdict and sentences were read. Richter, who had grinned at one point during the reading of the indictment last week, briefly appeared to blink away tears.

'Death threats' to widow alleged

Adrianos widow, Angelika, was not in court for the verdict. She decided to stay away after receiving death threats, said Razak Minhel, a liaison officer with the international community in the East German city of Dessau, where she lives with the couple's three children.

Adriano was walking home when the three set upon him, shouting racist abuse. They stripped him after he stopped moving. He died three days later, leaving behind a wife and three young sons.

Defence lawyer Sabine Grunow said all of the accused expressed regret in brief closing statements on the Friday after the four-day trial, which was closed to the public because it involved juveniles.

Adriano came to the then East Germany from Mozambique in the 1980s under a socialist worker exchange program and remained after unification, working in a meatpacking plant.

His death was one of three this year blamed on extreme-right attacks in Germany, a wave of violence that has prompted outrage and dismay among political leaders.

Brutal race-hate murder victim Alberto Adriano.

Chancellor Gerhard Schroeder has made the fight against neo-Nazi violence one of the focal points of his two-week tour through Germany's depressed former Communist eastern states, where recent attacks on foreigners have been concentrated.

He was to lay a wreath at a memorial marking the site where Adriano was beaten during a visit to Dessau on Thursday, government spokeswoman Charima Reinhardt said.

In a television interview on Wednesday, Schroeder reiterated his call for a 'triad' approach: toughness by police and the courts against perpetrators, better employment and training prospects for the 'young hangers-on' to pull them out of the neo-Nazi scene and 'societal engagement ... to stand up for what's right.'

'This is not just an east German problem, even if there are also especially dangerous characteristics that have to be fought decisively', he said on ARD television.

RELIGIONS IN GERMANY

The Reformation began in Germany when Martin Luther published his teachings in 1517. This religious challenge gave rise to Protestantism. By 1600, most people in northern and central Germany had become Protestants, mostly Lutherans. Those in the west and south remained Catholic.

Cologne's Gothic cathedral contains many art treasures. On the high altar are relics that are said to be those of the Magi, brought from Rome to Cologne in 1164.

In the 1970s the distributions of the Christian faiths was similar to above. About 50 per cent of West Germans were Protestants and about 80 per cent of East Germans were Protestants. The East German government tried to discourage religious practice. It tried to replace confirmation and other religious ceremonies for young people with ceremonies in which they dedicated themselves to Communism. Nevertheless, only 7 per cent of the East Germans at that time claimed to be non-religious.

In Germany today the percentages are different. In the former GDR (East Germany) less than a quarter, 25 per cent, of the population belongs to a religious community. In the West, the figure is 90 per cent. Germany's present population of over 80 million people may be divided into four religious groups.

The **Roman Catholic and Protestant churches each account for 30 per cent** of the population (2 x 30% = 60% of total population). **Another 30 per cent have non-religious affiliations.** The remaining 10 per cent are made up of approximately 3.3 million **Muslims**, who mostly live in the western region, 1.2 million **Orthodox Christians** (Eastern Orthodox Church) and about 1 million members each in free Christian churches and new religious movements. In addition there are 100,000 **Hindus**, 150,000 **Buddhists** and more than 150,000 people of the **Jewish faith**.

Basic Law of Germany guarantees full religious freedom and it provides protection against discrimination on religious grounds. A special feature of German law allows religious groups the possibility of collecting a church tax through public tax offices.

In other words it may be deducted from one's salary by the state and paid directly into church funds. However, for this to occur, German law states that there must be a church structure with an associated teaching body. This is not so with Islam. Muslims do not have such a church structure in Germany and so Islam does not have a public-body status and Islamic religious education is not yet permitted in state schools.

MUSIC IN GERMANY

Music plays a major role in German culture. Classical as well as traditional music are important.

Lutheran Churches follow the teachings of Martin Luther. He opposed the sale of indulgences and his beliefs led him to question many of the rules of the Christian church at that time.

Classical

Four of the most famous German classical composers include

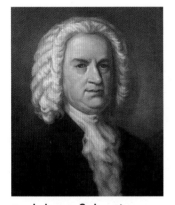   

- **Johann Sebastian Bach** spent most of his life in Leipzig working in the Lutheran church of St Thomas as a cantor, organist and composer.

- **Georg Friedrich Handel** started his career as a child performer on the piano. He worked as a musician and composer for Hamburg opera house.

- **Felix Mendelssohn** was another very successful musician, teacher and composer.

- **Richard Wagner** is mostly known for his opera music that was moving and powerful in its effects.

Traditional Music

The Munich Oktoberfest – known locally as the *Wiesen* is the biggest public festival in the world and was held in 2003 for the 170th time. Each year it attracts about 6 million visitors, who drink a total of about 5 million litres of beer and consume about 200,000 pairs of pork sausages, mostly in 'beer tents' put up by the traditional Munich breweries.

This famous festival attracts visitors from all over the world who spend about 1 billion euros during its sixteen days. About 12,000 people are employed to stage this festival.

The Oktober festival has continued for over 170 years.

SPORT IN GERMANY

Athletics is a popular sport. Many of Germany's athletes are Olympic champions.

An active sporting nation?

In 2001, the number of Germans who were members of the country's 87,000 sports clubs was estimated at 26.8 million – or one in three German citizens and an increase of 3 million people on the 1990 figure. The actual figure may be closer to 18 million German club members. However, some sportsmen and sportswomen belong to more than one club, whereas others are merely passive or social members.

This figure is even more impressive if you consider the fact that only 29 per cent of German sportsmen and sportswomen play their sports 'primarily in a club'. Fifty-eight per cent of people regularly participating in sport do not belong to any organisation i.e. they cycle or jog. Another 12 per cent use a commercial facility such as a fitness centre or a dance studio. In fact, the number of fitness centres has more than doubled since 1985, rising from 2,800 to 6,500.

According to a report commissioned by the Institut für Demoskopie in Allensbach in March 2001, 63 per cent of Germans claim to take part in sporting activities, and 34 per cent do so at least once a week.

The German government is becoming increasingly concerned about the health of the 37 per cent of Germans who do not take part in any sporting activity. Not least for financial reasons – medical research has shown lack of exercise and physical work to be one of the reasons for the increase in cardiovascular diseases, and about 30 per cent of medical costs incurred in Germany result from heart, circulatory or metabolic disorders.

This is a major problem in an ageing population, as 52 per cent of German adults who don't exercise are aged fifty or over, and only one in ten German adults between the age of thirty-five and sixty, does two hours or more of moderate sporting activity.

Soccer is a major sport in Germany. Every major town has a soccer club. The most famous German club is Bayern-Munich.

Skiing is a favourite sport in the Bavarian region of southern Germany. Its cold winters and heavy snowfalls make this mountainous region attractive as a skiing resort.

Roy Mackaay of Bayern Munich celebrates scoring the UEFA Championships League's winning goal.

The German soccer team of 2002.

Class activity

Explain how music is an important bonding influence within the German nation.

TEST YOURSELF AT
my-etest.com

Picture Credits

For permission to reproduce photographs and other material, the author and publisher gratefully acknowledge the following:

The author and publisher have made every effort to trace all copyright holders, but if any has been inadvertently overlooked we would be pleased to make the necessary arrangements at the first opportunity.